CELEBRITIES PRAISE
THE COMPASSIONATE COOK
OR, "PLEASE DON'T EAT THE ANIMALS!"
A VEGETARIAN COOKBOOK

"This splendid collection of recipes shows how you can have exciting, varied, and healthy meals without allowing your purchases to support the ruthless exploitation of sentient creatures."

—**Peter Singer,** author of *Animal Liberation*

"Opus told me that his six-year pickled-herring habit ended after reading *The Compassionate Cook*. He discovered the rutabaga frappé recipe and has been practicing it ever since. We both wish you Bon Appétit!"

—**Berke Breathed,** author of "Outland"
and "Bloom County" cartoons

"How good it is to be well-fed, healthy, and kind all at the same time."

—**Henry Heimlich, M.D., Sc.D.,**
president of The Heimlich Foundation

"What a great book . . . and such a wonderful cause! I look forward to trying each and every recipe."

—**Doris Day**

"I have always felt that the way we treat our animals is a pretty good indicator of the compassion we are capable of for the human race."

—**Ali MacGraw**

"Here the recipes will intrigue the most doubting of Thomases, and most of them are so imaginative and yet easy to prepare that even this old crotchety curmudgeon was inspired to dust off his cast-iron skillet and work up a stew."

—**Cleveland Amory,** author of *The Cat Who Came for Christmas*
and president of The Fund for Animals and NEAVS

"Leave it to PETA to publish a book full of answers for those who want to eat consciously and well."

—**Alec Baldwin**

"This is the book for people who care. It will be enjoyed by vegetarians and meat-eaters alike, because it helps us live a little lighter on the Earth."

—Dr. Michael W. Fox, D.V.M., and
author of *The New Animal Doctor's Answer Book*

"*The Compassionate Cook* is absolutely wonderful. There are so many recipes that I have been searching for but have been unable to find until now. Absolutely comprehensive and completely accessible."

—Sabrina LeBeauf, actor

"Abandon all fears that evolving towards a compassionate diet will be a tasteless journey. This rich collection of recipes from PETA is from people who not only love animals, but obviously love to eat. Accept their invitation to a delicioius world of nourishing, cruelty-free foods."

—Michael Klaper, M.D.,
author of *Vegan Nutrition: Pure and Simple*

"If you don't know how to get started, switching to a meatless diet can be a NIGHTMARE! Finally, here's a book that takes the HORROR out of what to eat when you don't eat meat."

—Cassandra Peterson, a.k.a. Elvira

"This is a terrific cookbook."

—Paul Obis, publisher
and editor-in-chief of *Vegetarian Times*

"I was a 'veggie junk-food junkie,' but delicious dishes like 'Tofu Scrambles' and 'Mock Chopped Liver' actually enticed me into the kitchen! These PETA recipes are not only good for our friends the animals, but good for us and tasty, too!"

—Jane Wiedlin, musician

"Anyone who still thinks of vegetarian cuisine as a bland, boring alternative to *real* food will be pleasantly surprised by *The Compassionate Cook*. And if good health and good intentions are part of the recipe—why not?"

—Paul Harvey, Jr., radio commentator

"When a person sits down to a vegetarian meal, that person is making a contribution to the better health of two individuals, him or herself on the one hand and the animal who was not killed on the other."

—Congressman Andrew Jacobs, Jr.

"If you wouldn't eat the family dog, you shouldn't eat the factory cow. This book is a delicious alternative for consistent, compassionate living. For all those who think vegetarianism means eating rocks and grass, this book is for you!"

—Sherry Ramsey and **Grant Aleksander,** actors

"Go vegan—make the world better for animals and human beings every time you eat. How? It's as easy as tofu pie with Ingrid Newkirk's recipes and tips. Get a healthy bod along with a meaningful life!"

—**Jim Mason,** co-author of *Animal Factories*

"PETA's cookbook is the best way I know for people to show that they care about animals. I use it every day I'm home!"

—**Rue McClanahan**

"What is this myth people hold that they get strength from eating the flesh of animals? I get my strength from letting them live."

—**Linnéa Quigley,** actor

"Sure to be a standby for vegetarian chefs, *The Compassionate Cook* is also an excellent resource for non-vegetarians (or not-yet-vegetarians) looking for ways to eat a little leaner, a little cleaner, a little kinder, and not sacrifice *anything* in the process."

—**Victoria Moran,** author of *The Love-Powered Diet*

"Ingrid's book offers delicious, healthy vegan recipes for those of us who love animals and love to eat . . . like me! A must for the experienced vegetarian and those trying to kick the meat habit! A 10+!"

—**Kevin Nealon**

"Inspirational. . . . The recipes reflect some of the best vegetarian cooking and prove, once again, that we can eat exciting, delicious, varied dishes without ever harming a single animal. *The Compassionate Cook* is a welcome addition to my cookbook shelf."

—**Jennifer Raymond,** vegetarian chef and author of
The Peaceful Palate: Fine Vegetarian Cuisine

"Feed your spirit as you feed your body! Blend a cup each of commitment and caring; mix in luscious vegetarian recipes. Yield: one compassionate cook. Liberating your kitchen has just become easier."

—**Carol Adams,** author of *The Sexual Politics of Meat*

"*The Compassionate Cook* will be a great resource for those who want to gratify their tastebuds without the help of fat- and cholesterol-laden meat, dairy, and egg foods."

—**Michael Jacobsen,** director,
Center for Science in the Public Interest

"*The Compassionate Cook* is perfect for anyone who wants to break the boring burger routine. You'll look and feel better, and the animals will thank you for it."

—**Tony La Russa,** manager,
Oakland A's, and Elaine La Russa

THE
COMPASSIONATE
COOK

or, "Please Don't Eat the Animals!"
A VEGETARIAN COOKBOOK

**PEOPLE FOR THE ETHICAL TREATMENT OF ANIMALS
AND INGRID NEWKIRK, NATIONAL DIRECTOR OF PETA**

WARNER BOOKS

A Time Warner Company

Copyright © 1993 by People for the Ethical Treatment of Animals and Ingrid Newkirk
All rights reserved.

Warner Books, Inc., 1271 Avenue of the Americas, New York, NY 10020
W A Time Warner Company

Printed in the United States of America
First Printing: July 1993
10 9 8 7 6 5 4

Cover design by Diane Luger
Cover illustration by Berkeley Breathed
Book design by L & G McRee
Book illustrations by Susan Hellard

Library of Congress Cataloging-in-Publication Data

The compassionate cook, or, "Please don't eat the animals!" : a
    vegetarian cookbook / People for the Ethical Treatment of Animals
    and Ingrid Newkirk.
        p.   cm.
    Includes index.
    ISBN 0-446-39492-0
    1. Vegetarian cookery.   I. Newkirk, Ingrid.   II. People for the
Ethical Treatment of Animals.
TX837.C593   1993
641.5'636—dc20   92-41804
                                                            CIP

This book was printed on recycled paper

"If slaughterhouses had glass walls, everyone would be vegetarian. We feel better about ourselves and better about the animals, knowing we're not contributing to their pain."

—PAUL AND LINDA McCARTNEY

ACKNOWLEDGMENTS

Thanks to the following PETA members, staff, family, and friends for contributing the recipes that make this cookbook kind to the animals and delicious to the tastebuds:

Dale Azaren; Amy Bertsch; Wanda Blake; Lori Bonner; Kym Boyman; David Cantor; Barbara A. Cassidy; Doug Claycomb; Ruth Dahl; Karen Davis; Becky DeLoach; Anita Dimino; Lydia Dorosh; Jan Downing; R. Duffy; Jeannie Dyar; Candace East; Katie Fisher; Audrey Foote; Teresa M. Geil; Heather Gray; Susan Gray; Jerry Houchens; Raj Jalali; Denis Jaricot; K. Joos; Robin Kaufer; Kathryn F. Klauda; Doris P. Krauch; Alicia LeClair; Susan Lehman; Mary Lovejoy; Robyn Mandell; Trysha Mapley; Gail Marine; Elizabeth McKay; Tricia Lilequist McNamara; David and Lori Miles; Liz Morgan; Linda Morse; Alisa Mullins; Roberta Mullins; Linda Nealon; Jeanne Neemajer; Ida Percoco; Robin Perry; Betty Porreca; Louise Porter; Mafalda Prete; Stephanie Prete; Magali Rojas; Lucinda Ross; Jeanne Roush; Lori Russler; Miriam C. Safford; Charles G. Santora; Jo-Ann Severa; Steven Simmons; JoAnne Smith; Kathy Spiros; Emily Stevenson; Debby Stirling; Wendy Thacher; Evelyn Thor; Susanne Ullmann; Nancy Vabre; Robin Walker; Michael Weaver; Uta Weckerle; Kathleen A. Welsh; Robyn Wesley; Norman and Judy Wilhoite.

Thanks, too, to the following volunteers and staff who made up PETA's Exclusive Tasters Club and who graciously spent many weeknights and weekends perfecting the wonderful dishes that fill these pages:

Jonathan Balcombe; Janet Beals; Beth Beck; Gardner Bennett; Karin Bennett; Amy Bertsch; David Cantor; Beth Ferris; Jyoti Jalali; Dan Mathews; Alisa Mullins; Ingrid Newkirk; Robin Perry; Karen Porreca; Martha Powers; Stephanie Prete; Mike Rodman; Jeanne Roush; Steven Simmons; Mary Beth Sweetland; Harald Ullmann; Nancy Vabre; Robin Walker; Uta Weckerle; and Robyn Wesley.

Special thanks also to Carla and Karin Bennett, Christine Jackson, Jyoti Jalali, Karen Porreca, Stephanie Prete and Robyn Wesley for helping make this dream book a reality.

CONTENTS

INTRODUCTION

Dear Reader,

Considering we are members of the primate family, most of us eat pretty peculiarly. You won't find gorillas and orangutans tossing unidentifiable animal parts on the grill. They're out in what's left of the rain forests and jungles, eating fresh, organic, locally grown foods that we might only hope to find in health food stores: fruits, vegetables, and nuts that make their hair shine, build phenomenally strong bodies, and help them stay enviably lithe and athletic.

Don't panic. This book isn't about recognizing edible plants, junking your oven, or gaining enough stamina to climb the Empire State Building. But it does offer something exciting: easy, delicious, healthy, and completely humane recipes for super veggie food that sometimes tastes exactly like, sometimes a lot like, and at other times nothing like the sort of eating most of us grew up with.

As a bonus, it is environmentally friendly and won't hurt your body or weigh you down as an animal-based diet can. And it's 100 percent fellow-creature-friendly.

At People for the Ethical Treatment of Animals (PETA), new staff members aren't always vegetarians when they join us. But watching ugly videos of exactly how pigs become wieners and chickens end up as batter-coated bird bits quickly turns the most addicted carnivores around. Others are switching to veggie meals because they want to lose weight; prevent cancers, stroke, and heart disease; stop supporting the environmental devastation caused by animal-based agriculture; fight world hunger; or live longer. For instance, vegetarian men live, on average, seven years longer than males who don't kick the meat habit.

Since 1980, PETA has been pleased to provide new vegetarians, whatever their reasons for making the change, with great recipes. Now, these recipes are collected for the first time in book form. Here's to a satisfied, healthy, and humane you!

INGRID NEWKIRK

1 A NOTE ABOUT NUTRITION

Vegetarian foods are not just good for all the animals you don't eat. They also are great for your waistline, your coronary arteries, and your longevity.

Grains, vegetables, fruits, and beans are very low in fat and high in complex carbohydrates, which boost your metabolism and improve your ability to burn calories. The result is weight control that is easier than any diet and, best of all, permanent. Vegetarians also tend to have healthier hearts. Because animal products are the only source of cholesterol and the main source of saturated fat in the diet, vegetarian foods are terrific for keeping a healthy heart. And, along with other parts of a healthy life-style (not smoking, daily exercise, stress reduction), vegetarian foods can actually make existing heart disease go away—something that is not possible with the lean meat, poultry, and fish diets that have been recommended in the past.

Plant-based diets help prevent cancer. Breast cancer, for example, occurs less often when people eat foods that are lower in fat and higher in fiber and certain vitamins. Cancers of the colon, prostate, and other organs are also strongly linked to foods, and a vegetarian diet is clearly best. A vegetarian diet is also great for children. While their meat-eating friends develop the beginnings of heart disease and start building their cancer risk, vegetarian children are safer on both counts.

Of course, the word *vegetarian* means different things to different people. The best diet is one that includes no animal products at all. This is called a pure vegetarian or vegan diet (pronounced *VEE-gun*). Vegans have the lowest cholesterol levels and all-around best health of any group. Ovo-lacto vegetarians consume eggs and milk, and get some benefits of a vegetarian diet, but not to the extent that vegans do.

Three concerns sometimes arise when people discuss vegetarian diets: protein, calcium, and vitamin B^{12}. Happily, all three are very easily addressed:

1. It was once thought that vegetarians would get enough protein only by carefully combining (or "complementing") certain foods, such as grains and beans. It is now known that any normal selection of plant foods provides more than enough protein, and intentional combining is not necessary. In fact, plant protein is better than animal protein for the body in several ways. It helps preserve kidney function and bone strength, and even helps lower cholesterol levels and cancer risk.

2. Calcium balance is actually easier to achieve on vegetarian diets than on meat diets. This is not just because green leafy vegetables and beans are rich in calcium. More important, meats cause a *wasting* of calcium from the body. Because of the amount and type of proteins in meats, calcium ends up being pulled from the bones and is excreted in the urine. Osteoporosis and hip fractures are epidemic in America and other Western countries, because of both the meat-based diet and the increasingly sedentary life-style.

3. Vitamin B^{12} is needed by the body in tiny amounts for healthy nerve function and blood. It is not made by animals or plants, but by single-celled life forms, such as bacteria. Bacteria on unwashed

vegetables and fermented products such as Asian miso and tempeh contain B^{12}, but in the hygienic modern world, these are not predictable sources. Animal products do contain B^{12} because animals have bacteria in their digestive tracts that produce the vitamin. But vegetarians can easily get B^{12} in their diet from fortified cereals and from vitamin supplements. All common vitamin supplements, including vegetarian vitamins, contain B^{12}.

When you eat vegetarian foods, not only will the animals thank you, your body will, too.

NEAL BARNARD, M.D.
President,
Physicians Committee for Responsible Medicine

2

WHAT TO EAT INSTEAD OF...

Why is it that we call some animals "pets" and others "dinner"? Millions of people care about animals, and everyone who cares about animals eats. Yet with some exceptions, even those who care about animals usually eat them regularly without even stopping to think twice about the process that brings once-vital and dear beings to the table. This book offers an alternative: an array of delicious and satisfying (even elegant!) recipes designed to help people be consistent in their compassion.

There are an estimated 8 to 9 million vegetarians in the United States, according to the North American Vegetarian Society. A 1991 Gallup poll commissioned by the National Restaurant Association revealed that 39 percent of those turning to vegetarianism are making the switch for ethical reasons. The same poll showed that about 20 percent of all American adults who eat out are "likely to look for a restaurant that serves vegetarian items," and that about a third are likely to order vegetarian meals. A report from the Food Marketing Institute notes that 31 percent of American supermarket shoppers say they are eating less meat, and 7 percent are eating fewer dairy products. That's why this book makes a great gift for someone with a kind heart, animals at home, or just a yen for new tastes, a longer life, and a healthier body.

A vegetarian life-style can save lives—yours and the animals'—as well as conserve the earth's precious resources of topsoil, water, and trees. PETA's first two books, *Save the Animals!* and *Kids Can Save the Animals!* provide more information on the reasons for and the benefits of a vegetarian diet, along with hundreds of other ways to help animals.

But once you've decided to lay off animals and animal products, what will you eat? If you're like most Americans, you are accustomed to meat and/or dairy products and eggs at nearly every meal. *The Compassionate Cook* will show you how easy it can be to switch to delicious, healthy, strictly vegetarian (sometimes called vegan) food. It provides 200 favorite recipes from our most experienced vegetarian cooks—PETA's dedicated (and food-loving) staff and members. With this book in hand, you'll be able to translate your respect for animals into daily action.

A good cookbook should inspire you to experiment with new dishes, cooking methods, and even ingredients. You will find that some of the recipes in this book have ingredients you've never used before, or in some cases, have never even heard of. Not every recipe has such ingredients, but you'll want to know where you can find soy milk, egg replacer, texturized vegetable protein (TVP), eggless mayonnaise, or silken tofu. Check the Glossary of Ingredients (page 227) for information on unfamiliar products. You will also find that many of the recipes in this cookbook call for little or no added oil. When you do use oil, we recommend using unrefined vegetable oils or olive oil. It is best to use oil sparingly as it imparts a lot of fat and calories and is hard on your heart. Water can be substituted when sautéing foods. Unrefined vegetable oils are available in health food stores. You can also find Sucanat in many health food stores. Sucanat is organically grown granulated sugar cane juice, which is completely unrefined. We recommend using Sucanat in any recipe that calls for sugar.

Fortunately, most large supermarkets now have a health food or "diet" section where you'll find things like meat substitutes, egg replacer (Ener G Foods is a common brand), and dairy-free baked goods. Also, check out the "international" section, if your store has one, for things like refried beans without lard and less common kinds of beans. (Shops that specialize in ethnic foods, often located alongside restaurants, are also worth looking into.) You can often find tofu in one-pound packages in the produce section, although some tofu comes in 10-ounce packages that don't require refrigeration and are sold in most health food stores.

Health food stores usually carry a multitude of other meatless and dairyless wonders, such as soy "hot dogs," TVP, soy milk, and "ice cream" in a variety of convincing flavors; as well as grains you might not find in your local supermarket, like millet and bulgur, organic produce, and nutritional yeast. Check the glossary for advice on shopping for specific ingredients.

Once you become familiar with using foods like egg replacer, tofu, and nutritional yeast, you'll have fun—and success!—adapting your favorite recipes from their old high-fat, high-cholesterol versions to new lower-fat, no-cholesterol dishes. Maybe you already replace butter with margarine or reduce the amount of cooking oil you use; other adaptations and substitutions are just as easy and even more beneficial to health. You can "brown" crumbled tofu in a pan just as you would ground beef or "scramble" it like eggs with onion, green pepper, mushrooms, and spices. You'll find that cookies, muffins, and other baked goods come out just as well when you use margarine, soy milk, and egg replacer or tofu instead of the usual dairy-and-egg pairing. In this book you'll find recipes to replace some of the standards on your menu, such as Spanish omelettes, lasagna, and cheesecake.

Even when you're eating out, you can apply some of the same strategies. In an Italian restaurant, order pasta with tomato or marinara sauce. You often can get salsa in place of butter or sour cream for a baked potato, or in place of a yogurt-based dip with a platter of raw vegetables. Even restaurants that list no vegetarian entrees on their menus often are willing to accommodate customers who ask for vegetable plates or who order two or three appetizers rather than a conventional meal. Many ethnic restaurants have a meatless entree, or even a selection of them. Check out Chinese, Thai, Indian, Ethiopian, and Middle Eastern places.

If you're going to a friend's or relative's house for lunch, dinner, or an overnight visit, let her or him know ahead of time of your dietary principles. Offer to bring a dish to share or, if your host seems amenable, offer a sampling of recipes in advance or suggest ways to adapt the planned dish to one that you can share. If you're going to be at someone's house for several days, offer to prepare (or assist with the preparation of) a breakfast or dinner. This way, you can introduce people you care about to a more healthful and humane way of eating, as well as give your host a break.

If the shoe is on the other foot, and you're expecting guests who are accustomed to eating meat every day, explain why your chosen diet is important to you, and encourage them to be open-minded about the meatless meals you'll prepare for them. You might consider taking them to a favorite restaurant, where they can choose what sounds good to them and maybe get a taste of something they've never had before, such as Thai or Ethiopian food.

The Russian novelist Leo Tolstoy, a committed vegetarian, wrote in *The First Step*, "And how deeply seated in the human heart is the injunction not to take life! But . . . as a result of habit, people entirely lose their natural feeling." As you try the recipes in this book, you will be amazed not only at how easy it is to switch to an animal-friendly diet but also how varied, enjoyable, and satisfying a vegetarian diet can be. And your friends and family will compliment you on your new culinary expertise. You will also be delighted by the change you experience in yourself—rediscovered energy since you'll be eating lighter, and a recaptured "natural feeling" since you'll know that your body is no longer dependent on once-living beings.

3

GREAT BEGINNINGS

"Vegetarianism is a link to
perfection and peace."
—RIVER PHOENIX

The typical bacon-and-eggs breakfast is eggs-tremely hazardous to
your health. Consider this: two eggs (also known as up to 500
milligrams of cholesterol) can raise your blood cholesterol by about 25
points and increase your risk of heart attack by 12 percent. Who needs
it? This chapter is full of delicious, healthful alternatives to break the
fat- and cholesterol-laden greasy routine.

Many nutritionists agree that breakfast is the most important meal of
the day. You can boost your energy level by getting a nutritious start.
Eat a breakfast packed with power, such as a bowl of hot or cold
cereal and soy milk, a quick fruit shake, or soy links with a bagel. On

the pages that follow, you'll find quick and easy recipes that will have
you off and running in no time.

On your days off, sleep in! Then saunter into the kitchen and start
cooking. Treat everyone in the house to a leisurely brunch, including
fresh fruit and tofu spread on bagels, hot pancakes smothered in pure
maple syrup, and tasty bean sausages. Slow down and savor the
delectable flavors.

PANCAKES

*You'll become a crackerjack flapjack maker when you try this recipe.
For an added treat, toss bits of fresh or dried fruit, nuts, or chocolate
chips into the batter.*

1   **cup unbleached all-purpose flour**
1   **tablespoon sugar**
2   **tablespoons baking powder**
⅛   **teaspoon salt**
1   **cup soy milk**
2   **tablespoons vegetable oil**

Combine the flour, sugar, baking powder, and salt in a bowl and mix
thoroughly. Mix in the soy milk and oil, and with an electric mixer or
wire whisk, beat just until the batter is smooth.

Measure ⅓ cup batter onto a hot, oiled griddle. When bubbles appear
on the upper surface of the pancake, in about 2 minutes, lift with a
spatula and flip the pancake. Cook the pancake for another 2 minutes.
Remove from pan and keep warm while you make remaining pancakes. Serve warm with maple syrup or fruit syrup.

Makes 6 to 8 pancakes   PREPARATION TIME: 45 minutes

FRENCH TOAST

This is guaranteed to get them out of bed.

1½ **cups soy milk**
2   **tablespoons unbleached all-purpose flour**
1   **tablespoon nutritional yeast**
1   **teaspoon sugar**
1   **teaspoon ground cinnamon**
1   **tablespoon vegetable oil**
4–6 **slices bread (thick-sliced crusty white or wheat bread)**

Mix the soy milk, flour, yeast, sugar, and cinnamon vigorously with a wire whisk or beater. Pour the mixture into a wide, shallow bowl or pie pan.

Heat the oil in a frying pan or skillet. Dip a bread slice into the mixture and then place in skillet. Fry each side until golden brown and crispy, about 5 to 7 minutes total. Remove from pan and keep warm while cooking remaining slices.

Serve hot with maple syrup.

Serves 2   PREPARATION TIME: 20 minutes

TOFU SCRAMBLES

You'll have brunch guests scrambling for more of this delish, eggless dish, so you might want to cook up a double batch.

1   **pound firm tofu, patted dry and mashed**
⅛   **teaspoon turmeric**
1   **teaspoon onion powder**
½   **teaspoon salt**
1   **cup finely chopped vegetables (green bell pepper, fresh mush-**
      rooms, onions, tomatoes—whatever you like)

Place the tofu in a lightly oiled sauté pan and cook over medium for 3 minutes. Add the remaining ingredients, stir well, and cook for 5 to 8 minutes, until the vegetables are cooked and the tofu is heated through.

Serves 4   PREPARATION TIME: 15 minutes

SPANISH TOFU OMELETTE

Enjoy a healthier classic—a savory omelette packed with flavor, not cholesterol.

1   **tablespoon olive oil or water**
1   **clove garlic, minced**
1   **small onion, chopped**
1   **medium potato, sliced**
¼   **green bell pepper, diced**
1   **small tomato, chopped**
¼   **teaspoon dried oregano**
1   **pound soft tofu, patted dry**
¼   **cup unbleached all-purpose flour**
¼   **teaspoon turmeric**
1   **teaspoon nutritional yeast**
Salt and pepper to taste

In a frying pan over medium heat, heat the oil or water and sauté the garlic, onion, potato, and green pepper until the potato is cooked, about 10 minutes.

In the meantime, blend the remaining ingredients in a blender until smooth. Add the tomato and tofu mixture to the pan and cook, covered, over a very low heat until the omelette is set, about 10 minutes.

Serve with salsa.

Serves 4   PREPARATION TIME: 30 minutes

APPLESAUCE-BRAN BREAKFAST CAKE

Even the sleepiest of sleepyheads won't be able to resist this cake. The ingredients can be measured and ready to go the night before, then quickly mixed and baked in the morning.

¼   **cup (½ stick) margarine**
2   **cups applesauce, sweetened or unsweetened**
1   **cup unbleached all-purpose flour**
1½ **cups unprocessed wheat bran flakes or oat bran**
1   **cup sugar**
1   **teaspoon baking soda**
1   **teaspoon ground cinnamon**
½   **teaspoon grated nutmeg**
¼   **teaspoon ground cloves**
1   **cup raisins**
1   **cup chopped nuts**

Preheat the oven to 350 degrees. Grease the *bottom only* of a 9-inch square baking pan.

In a large saucepan, heat the margarine and applesauce together over medium heat until the margarine is just melted, then remove from heat. Add the remaining ingredients, stir quickly to moisten, then pour the batter into the baking pan. Bake for 25 to 30 minutes, or until a toothpick inserted in the center comes out clean.

Serves 6   PREPARATION TIME: 10 minutes
                              BAKING TIME: 25–30 minutes

EASY FRUIT TURNOVERS

Fruit-filled turnovers are an easy treat that kids love!

½ recipe Sister's Pie Crust recipe (p. 188)
Your favorite fruit preserve

Preheat the oven to 450 degrees.

Divide the dough into 4 equal parts. On a floured board, roll each section into a small 5-inch circle with a rolling pin. Drop 2 tablespoons of preserves into the center of each circle and spread on dough up to within 1 inch of edge of circle.

Fold the dough over into half-moons. Turn the edges up and press with a fork to seal. Bake for 15 minutes, or until the crust is golden. Let cool completely before serving.

Serves 4   PREPARATION TIME: 25 minutes
                              BAKING TIME: 15 minutes

SMOKY, CRUNCHY BREAKFAST TEMPEH

No need to bring home the bacon; bring home the tempeh instead.

1 tablespoon vegetable oil
8 ounces tempeh, sliced very thin

2 teaspoons Liquid Smoke
3 teaspoons soy sauce or tamari

In a sauté pan, heat the oil until quite hot.
    Add the tempeh slices and fry on both sides until brown and crispy.
Add the Liquid Smoke and tamari (be careful—the oil may splatter).
Turn the tempeh over and cook for another minute.

Serves 2 to 4   PREPARATION TIME: 20 minutes

NO-PORK SAUSAGE

*Since this "sausage" has all the flavor but none of the cholesterol of
the real thing, your whole family will want to indulge!*

1   10-ounce package frozen lima beans, thawed
¾   cup Vegetable Broth (p. 52)
¼   teaspoon ground dried sage
¼   teaspoon dried rosemary leaves, crumbled
6   tablespoons cornmeal
1–2 tablespoons vegetable oil

In a blender or food processor, coarsely chop the lima beans with the
vegetable stock. The lima beans should remain chunky.
    In a medium saucepan, heat the lima bean mixture, sage, and
rosemary until boiling. Slowly beat in 4 tablespoons of the cornmeal
and cook until thickened and bubbly. Cool to room temperature.
    Sprinkle the rest of the cornmeal onto a pie plate. Pat the lima bean
mixture into ¼-inch patties and coat each patty with some of the
cornmeal on the pie plate. In a large skillet, heat 1 tablespoon of oil
and fry the patties until lightly crisped and browned on both sides,
about 5 minutes. Add more oil if necessary.

Serves 6   PREPARATION TIME: 45 minutes

HOT CHOCOLATE

Wondering how you'll ever get the kids to shovel all that snow in the driveway? Heat up some hot chocolate and they'll be too toasty to stay inside.

½ cup unsweetened cocoa powder
½ cup sugar
Dash of salt
½ cup water
6   cups vanilla soy milk
Tofu Whipped Cream (p. 222)
Cinnamon sticks (optional)

In a 2-quart saucepan, stir together the cocoa, sugar, and salt until well blended. Add the water and stir until smooth. Cook the mixture over medium heat until boiling, stirring constantly with a spoon or wire whisk. Lower the heat and cook 2 minutes more, stirring constantly.

Stir in the soy milk and heat until tiny bubbles form around the edge, stirring constantly. Remove the pan from the heat. Beat with a wire whisk or electric mixer until smooth and foamy, then pour into 8-ounce mugs.

Top with whipped tofu and garnish with cinnamon sticks.

Serves 6   PREPARATION TIME: 20 minutes

TOFU-FRUIT SPREAD

Yum! Whoever said bagels are boring?

2   sweet apples, peeled, cored, and chopped
2   ripe medium bananas, peeled and sliced
½ pound soft tofu, drained and crumbled

½ **teaspoon ground cinnamon**
1 **whole clove**
⅛ **teaspoon grated nutmeg**

Combine all the ingredients in a blender or food processor and blend until smooth. Chill. Spread on top of your morning bagel or toast.

Makes 4 servings   PREPARATION TIME: 10 minutes

STREUSEL COFFEE CAKE

A sophisticated, sweet, and wonderful way to start your Sunday.

Reprinted with permission from The Peaceful Palate: Fine Vegetarian Cuisine *by Jennifer Raymond.*

1   **cup soy milk**
1   **tablespoon distilled white vinegar**
⅓   **cup soft tofu**
2¼ **cups unbleached all-purpose flour or whole wheat pastry flour**
1¼ **cups packed light brown sugar**
3   **teaspoons ground cinnamon**
1½ **teaspoons ground ginger**
½   **teaspoon salt**
¾   **cup vegetable oil**
¾   **cup chopped walnuts**
1   **teaspoon baking powder**
1   **teaspoon baking soda**

Preheat the oven to 350 degrees. Grease a 9 × 13-inch baking dish.
    Place the soy milk, vinegar, and tofu in a blender and blend until completely smooth.
    In a large bowl, mix the flour, brown sugar, 2½ teaspoons of

cinnamon, ginger, salt, and oil. Work the mixture with a pastry knife, a fork, or your fingers until well blended. Transfer 1¼ cups of this mixture to a small bowl and mix in the remaining ½ teaspoon cinnamon and the walnuts. Set aside.

To the remaining flour mixture, add the baking powder and baking soda, along with the blended tofu. Mix until smooth. Spread the batter evenly in the baking dish and sprinkle the reserved flour-nut mixture over the top. Bake for 30 to 35 minutes, or until a cake tester inserted in the center comes out clean.

Serves 12

PREPARATION TIME: 30 minutes
BAKING TIME: 30–35 minutes

PEANUT BUTTER COFFEE CAKE

Serve this delight at your next brunch and it will be gone before your guests can say, "Another cup of java, please!"

Topping

½ cup packed light brown sugar
½ cup unbleached all-purpose flour
¼ cup peanut butter
3 tablespoons margarine

Cake

2¼ cups unbleached all-purpose flour
1 cup packed brown sugar
2 teaspoons baking powder
½ teaspoon baking soda
¼ teaspoon salt

1   cup soy milk
½   cup peanut butter
Egg replacer equivalent of 2 eggs
¼   cup (½ stick) margarine

Preheat the oven to 375 degrees. Grease a 9 × 13-inch baking pan.

For the topping, mix the brown sugar and flour. With a pastry knife, a fork, or your fingers, cut in the peanut butter and margarine until crumbly; set aside.

For the cake, combine the flour, brown sugar, baking powder, baking soda, and salt. Add the soy milk, peanut butter, egg replacer, and margarine. Beat until smooth, about 3 minutes with an electric mixer. Pour into baking pan and sprinkle with the topping.

Bake for 30 minutes, or until a toothpick inserted in the center comes out clean.

Serves 12   PREPARATION TIME: 20 minutes
                                      BAKING TIME: 30 minutes

4 PACKING LUNCH WITH A PUNCH

"One person can make all the difference in the world....For the first time in recorded human history, we have the fate of our whole planet in our hands....It's a very exciting time for vegetarians."

—CHRISSIE HYNDE

In most cases, it won't take any more time or effort to prepare the lunches in this chapter than it takes to slather some peanut butter and grape jelly on a couple of pieces of bread, but you will reap rewards in flavor by exercising your imagination muscle (with a little help from us). Try the hummus, for instance, for a spicy change from sandwich standbys.

The following lunch recipes benefit not only your taste buds but your waistline and arteries as well. They keep you from falling into the fast-food trap of high-fat, on-the-go meals like burgers, fries, and shakes. Unlike meals with a high sugar content, these hearty lunches keep you revved until dinnertime. And on rainy or windy winter days, when others in your office are complaining about having to go out for a bite, you can savor *your* lunch in toasty comfort.

SALADS AND SANDWICHES

TEMPEH SANDWICH SPREAD

Okay, so it sounds a little weird—a cultured soybean and grain cake. But we guarantee that, if you try it, you're going to love *it! Tempeh is savored by vegetarians who want to continue to enjoy the flavor and texture of meat while going veggie. It is available at health food and Oriental food stores.*

Reprinted with permission from The Peaceful Palate: Fine Vegetarian Cuisine *by Jennifer Raymond.*

8	**ounces tempeh**
3	**tablespoons Eggless Mayonnaise (p. 85)**
2	**teaspoons prepared mustard**
2	**green onions, chopped**
1–2	**stalks celery, finely chopped**
1	**tablespoon sweet pickle relish**

Steam the tempeh for 20 minutes. Allow to cool, then grate it and mix with the remaining ingredients. Cover and chill. Serve on a bed of crisp lettuce or use as a sandwich filling.

Serves 4   PREPARATION TIME: 30 minutes

EGGLESS EGG SALAD

Did you know the average egg contains a whopping 200 to 250 milligrams of cholesterol? Our eggless egg salad has all the flavor of the favorite without a smidgen of cholesterol.

1½   pounds firm tofu, mashed
½   cup Eggless Mayonnaise (p. 85)
½   cup chopped fresh parsley
¼   cup sweet pickle relish
½   medium onion, chopped
2   stalks celery, chopped
1½   teaspoons garlic powder
1½   teaspoons salt
¼   teaspoon turmeric
1½   tablespoons prepared mustard

Combine all the ingredients in a large bowl. Spread on sandwiches or crackers.

Serves 6   PREPARATION TIME: 10 minutes

AVOCADO REUBEN

Hold the cheese, please! Creamy avocados are spreadably, edibly delicious, and have zero cholesterol.

2   slices rye or pumpernickel bread
Mustard
Thousand Island dressing (p. 84)
½   avocado, pitted, peeled, and mashed
¼   cup sauerkraut

Spread one slice of bread with some mustard, the other with dressing. Lightly oil a frying pan and place the bread slices, dry side down, in the frying pan. Top one slice with avocado, and the other with sauerkraut. Over medium heat, grill the sandwich until lightly browned and hot, about 5 minutes. Put the halves together, slice in half, and enjoy!

Makes 1 sandwich   PREPARATION TIME: 15 minutes

HUMMUS

Just mix the ingredients and serve with pita bread and your favorite salad veggies for a satisfying lunch or supper.

2   **cloves garlic**
2   **cups cooked chickpeas, drained**
4   **tablespoons lemon juice**
½   **teaspoon salt**
3   **tablespoons tahini**
2   **tablespoons water**
Paprika
Olive oil

Combine the first 6 ingredients in a blender or food processor and blend until smooth. Add a little more water if needed to create a smooth paste. Transfer the hummus to a small serving dish, sprinkle with paprika and drizzle with olive oil, and use as dip. Or make sandwiches with pita pockets and your favorite veggies.

Makes 2 cups   PREPARATION TIME: 10 minutes

WALNUT CURRY SALAD

Who says salad has to be green to be good—and good for you? This tofu-based dish uses a surprising blend of flavors and textures.

1 **pound firm tofu, frozen and thawed**
⅓ **cup commercial Italian salad dressing**
1 **tablespoon mild curry powder**
¼ **teaspoon black pepper**
¼ **teaspoon salt**
1 **small onion, chopped**
3 **stalks celery, chopped**
1 **cup chopped walnuts**
Lettuce

Squeeze the excess water out of the thawed tofu and cut it into ¼-inch cubes. In a large mixing bowl, pour the dressing over the tofu. Add the remaining ingredients except lettuce and mix with a large spoon or spatula. Chill for at least 1 hour.

Serve salad on a bed of lettuce or with lettuce in a sandwich. If the salad becomes dry in the refrigerator, mix in a tablespoon of dressing before serving.

Serves 6   PREPARATION TIME: 15 minutes
                              CHILLING TIME: 1 hour

CHICKPEA SPREAD

Sure to become a lunchtime favorite, this tasty spread is a cinch to make. It's great in a pita pocket with your favorite veggies.

1 **cup cooked chickpeas, drained and mashed**
½ **stalk celery, finely chopped**
1 **tablespoon finely chopped onion**
1½ **tablespoons Eggless Mayonnaise (p. 85)**
½ **teaspoon prepared mustard**
½ **teaspoon lemon juice**
Salt and pepper to taste

Mix all the ingredients in a bowl. Add salt and pepper to taste.

Serves 4 to 6   · PREPARATION TIME: 10 minutes

CURRIED CHICKPEA PITA POCKETS

Great for lunch or a casual supper, this is an easy but satisfying recipe.

2   **tablespoons olive oil or water**
2   **medium onions, sliced**
2   **cloves garlic, crushed**
1   **teaspoon cumin powder**
1   **teaspoon turmeric**
1   **green bell pepper, sliced**
2   **stalks celery, chopped**
¼   **cup sliced fresh mushrooms**
4   **firm tomatoes, chopped**
2   **teaspoons chopped fresh coriander (cilantro)**
1   **15-ounce can chickpeas, drained**
4   **pita pockets, halved**

In a frying pan, heat the olive oil or water and sauté the onion and garlic for about 2 minutes. Stir in the cumin and turmeric. Add the green pepper and sauté a few minutes longer, stirring constantly. Add the celery, mushrooms, and tomatoes and stir well. Cook for another minute, then sprinkle the coriander on top. Stir the chickpeas into the mixture, reduce the heat, and cook for 5 minutes. Spoon the chickpea mixture into each pita pocket and serve.

Serves 4   PREPARATION TIME: 25 minutes

TEMPEH-HERB SANDWICH

Need a power lunch in a bag? Here's a hearty alternative to P.B. and J. (The power tie is optional.) If desired, use sandwich veggies in place of the sprouts.

8   ounces tempeh, cut into 1-inch squares
1   teaspoon vegetable oil
2   tablespoons Eggless Mayonnaise (p. 85)
2   tablespoons soy sauce or tamari
1   tablespoon minced onion
2   tablespoons dried parsley
¼   cup minced red bell pepper
¼   cup minced celery
⅛   teaspoon cayenne pepper
6–8   slices wheat bread
Lettuce
Sprouts

To steam tempeh: bring a medium-sized pot of water to a boil. Reduce heat to low, add tempeh and simmer for 15 minutes, then drain well.

Heat the oil in a skillet over medium-high heat and add the tempeh. Sauté for 5 minutes, stirring often. Transfer the tempeh to a bowl and add the mayonnaise, soy sauce or tamari, onion, parsley, red pepper, celery, and cayenne pepper. Mash the mixture well.

Spread on slices of bread and add lettuce and sprouts.

Makes 3 to 4 sandwiches   PREPARATION TIME: 25 minutes

MUSHROOM AND TOMATO TOAST

Low in fat and calories but big on taste, this is lunchtime perfection!

4 slices wheat bread
1 tablespoon margarine
2 medium tomatoes, sliced
1 cup sliced fresh mushrooms
Salt and pepper to taste
Nutritional yeast flakes (optional)

Preheat the oven to 300 degrees.
   Toast the bread, and set aside.
   In a small frying pan, melt the margarine over medium heat. Add the tomatoes and mushrooms, and sauté until soft, about 4 minutes. Add salt and pepper to taste.
   Place a little of the tomato-mushroom mixture on each piece of toast. Sprinkle with the yeast flakes and heat for 2 minutes in an oven. Serve immediately.

Serves 2 to 4   PREPARATION TIME: 15 minutes

BURGERS AND PUPS

VEGETABLE HOT DOGS IN BLANKETS

An oinker-free pup in a puff that'll leave you and the kiddies stuffed. Seasoned taste buds will savor Dijon mustard spread inside the dough before baking, an old French sausage vendor's trick.

1   17¼-ounce package puff pastry dough
12 tofu hot dogs

Preheat the oven to 425 degrees.

Roll out the dough to a ¼-inch thickness. Cut into twelve 3 × 5-inch rectangles. Wrap each tofu hot dog lengthwise in a piece of pastry dough and seal the edges with water. Place seam side down on a baking sheet and bake for 8 to 10 minutes.

Serves 6 to 12   PREPARATION TIME: 10 minutes

                          BAKING TIME: 8–10 minutes

TONY AND ELAINE LA RUSSA'S TOFU-ONION BURGERS

The first family of baseball's favorite burger is this veggie specialty. It's so good with Creamy Coleslaw (p. 74) and Oven-Fried Potatoes (p. 177).

½   **pound firm tofu, mashed well**
1   **medium onion, chopped very fine**
2   **tablespoons wheat germ**
2   **tablespoons unbleached all-purpose flour**
2   **teaspoons garlic powder**
2   **tablespoons soy sauce or tamari**
Pepper to taste
Oil for frying

Mix all the ingredients except oil in a bowl and form into patties. Heat a little oil in a skillet and fry patties until very brown and crisp, about 10 minutes. Serve these burgers on buns or as patties with a sauce.

Makes 4 patties   PREPARATION TIME: 20 minutes

LENTIL-CARROT BURGERS

Fire up that frying pan and clear up any misconceptions that natural foods are bland! Serve on a bun with tomato and sprouts.

¼ **cup finely chopped onion**
¼ **cup grated carrots**
¼ **cup water**
3 **cups cooked lentils, mashed**
2 **tablespoons chopped fresh parsley**
3 **tablespoons tomato paste**
¾ **cup bread crumbs**
Salt to taste
Oil for frying

Cook the onion and carrot in the water until tender, about 10 minutes. Drain off excess water, then combine the onion and carrot with the remaining ingredients except oil. Form into patties and fry in a lightly oiled frying pan until browned on both sides and heated through, about 10 minutes.

Makes 10 patties   PREPARATION TIME: 25 minutes

SLOPPY JOES

This sloppy joe filling is so easy to prepare, you'll have time to make a super salad to go with it or whip up a great dessert.

2 **tablespoons margarine (¼ stick) or water**
½ **cup minced onion**
½ **cup minced green bell pepper**

1   **pound firm tofu, patted dry and mashed**
6   **tablespoons ketchup**
6   **tablespoons chili sauce**
½   **teaspoon salt**
Pepper to taste
4   **burger buns, lightly toasted**

Heat the margarine or water in a large skillet over medium heat. Add the onion and green pepper, and sauté or boil until the vegetables are well cooked, about 5 minutes. Add the mashed tofu and sauté for another 15 minutes, until the tofu is completely cooked.

Add the ketchup, chili sauce, salt, and pepper and continue to cook over low heat until the mixture is heated through. Add a little water if mixture is too dry.

Spoon onto lightly toasted burger buns.

Serves 4   PREPARATION TIME: 30 minutes

5

SNACKS AND APPETIZERS

"Animals are my friends...and I don't eat my friends."
—George Bernard Shaw

Vegetarianism leads us to broaden our hors d'oeuvre repertoire, introducing a multitude of new treats. Mushroom and other pâtés, artichoke puff pastries, and an avocado and papaya salad will look as good as they taste. Savory Indian pastries like pakoras, and Middle Eastern baba ghanoush bring exotic flavors into play. And the ever-popular dips are sure to please everyone. Who won't love these delicacies? They'll perk up any party.

PÂTÉS

MUSHROOM-WALNUT PÂTÉ IN BELL PEPPER RINGS

Hide these until serving time, or they'll be gone.

¼ cup water
¾ pound sliced fresh mushrooms
½ medium onion, sliced
2   cloves garlic, minced
¼ pound firm tofu, mashed
½ cup walnuts
¼ teaspoon salt
¼ teaspoon black pepper
1   green bell pepper, cored and seeded
½ loaf of French bread

Heat the water in a medium frying pan over medium heat, then cook the mushrooms, onion, and garlic until soft, about 5 minutes. Put the vegetables and tofu in a food processor or blender and puree until smooth. Add the walnuts, salt, and pepper, and puree for another 5 minutes.

Chill the pâté thoroughly. Slice the bell pepper into rings, arrange on a plate on thinly sliced crusty French bread, and fill the rings with the pâté.

Serves 6 to 8   PREPARATION TIME: 20 minutes
                                   CHILLING TIME: 1 hour

MOCK CHOPPED LIVER

What do you think this is—chopped liver? Well, actually, it's much tastier and way better for you than the real thing.

1 tablespoon vegetable oil or water
1 large onion, sliced
1 pound green beans, trimmed
1 pound soft tofu
1 teaspoon paprika
Salt and pepper to taste

Heat the oil or water in a medium frying pan over medium heat. Cook the onion, stirring occasionally, until soft, about 5 minutes.

Steam the green beans over boiling water until just tender, about 10 minutes.

Place the onion, beans, and remaining ingredients in a food processor and puree until smooth. Transfer to a serving dish and chill for 4 hours or overnight.

Serve with crackers or toast.

Makes 4 cups   PREPARATION TIME: 30 minutes
                                  CHILLING TIME: 4 hours

VEGETABLE NUT PÂTÉ

A savory spread that's sure to become a mainstay on your party platters.

1 tablespoon vegetable oil or water
1 large onion
1 cup green beans, trimmed
1 cup cashews
1 tablespoon lemon juice
Salt and pepper to taste

Heat the oil or water in a small frying pan. Cook the onion slowly over moderately low heat, stirring frequently, until very soft, about 5–7 minutes.

Steam the green beans over boiling water until just tender, about 10 minutes.

Place the onion, beans, and the remaining ingredients in a food processor and puree until smooth. Transfer the pâté to a serving bowl and serve immediately. The pâté can be refrigerated, but bring it to room temperature before serving.

Makes 2 cups   PREPARATION TIME: 20 minutes

CRUELTY-FREE PÂTÉ

For a paste with taste, try this veggie version on plain crackers, toast, even rice cakes. Or if you want to really make an impression, bake the pâté in a puff pastry shell.

1   **medium onion, chopped**
1   **tablespoon margarine or water**
2   **pounds fresh mushrooms, finely chopped**
4   **cloves garlic, minced**
2   **tablespoons chopped fresh parsley, or 2 teaspoons dried**
2   **tablespoons chopped fresh rosemary, or 2 teaspoons dried**
1⅓   **cups bread crumbs**
2   **tablespoons lemon juice**
Salt and pepper

In a large saucepan, heat the margarine or water and cook the onion for 10 minutes.

Add the mushrooms and cook for another 20 to 30 minutes, or until all the liquid has evaporated. Remove the mixture from the heat and add the remaining ingredients. Spoon into a serving dish and serve immediately.

Variation: To bake the pâté in a puff pastry shell, preheat the oven to 425 degrees. Roll 1 pound of commercial puff pastry dough into two 6 × 12-inch rectangles. Line a baking sheet with one piece of dough and pile the mixture on top. Top with the other piece of dough and press the edges together to form a tight seal. Brush the dough with soy milk and bake for 30 minutes. Serve warm.

Serves 6   PREPARATION TIME: 20 minutes
                              BAKING TIME: 30 minutes (optional)

HOT APPETIZERS

SWEET POTATO PUFFS

Give your guests one bite of these puffs and poof—they'll disappear! (The puffs, not your guests. You're stuck with them for at least three more hours.)

1¼ **pounds sweet potatoes, peeled**
6   **tablespoons soy milk**
Salt and pepper to taste
2   **10-ounce packages frozen puff pastry shells (12 shells)**

Bake the sweet potatoes for 30 minutes, then puree with the soy milk and salt and pepper. Meanwhile, bake the pastry shells according to package directions.

Take the pastry shells from the oven, remove the tops, and fill with the warm sweet potato mixture. Replace the tops and serve immediately.

Makes 12 sweet potato puffs   PREPARATION TIME: 30 minutes
                                     BAKING TIME: 10 minutes

ARTICHOKE PUFFS

These puffs will be gone in minutes, but you'll be hearing raves about them for days!

2   **10-ounce packages puff pastry shells (12 shells)**
1   **teaspoon margarine**
2   **teaspoons water**
¼   **cup finely chopped onion or green onions**
2   **teaspoons cornstarch**
1¼ **cups soy milk**
1   **14-ounce can artichoke hearts**
Paprika
Salt and pepper to taste

Bake the pastry shells according to package directions until golden.

While the shells are baking, heat the margarine and water in a frying pan over medium heat. Cook the onion for 10 minutes, or until transparent. Stir in the cornstarch and continue cooking for 1 to 2 minutes. Add the soy milk and stir until thickened. Remove the pan from the heat and set aside.

Drain the artichoke hearts and chop coarsely. Add to the creamed mixture and season with the paprika, salt, and pepper.

Remove the tops from the pastry shells. Spoon the artichoke mixture into each pastry shell and reheat the puffs at 350 degrees for 5 minutes.

Replace the tops and serve immediately.

Serves 6 to 12   PREPARATION TIME: 10 minutes
                                    BAKING TIME: 25 minutes

HOT AND SPICY CASHEW NUTS

This recipe makes a great gift for the nut lover on your list.

8 cups water
1 teaspoon salt
4 slices fresh ginger
8 dried chili peppers
2 teaspoons curry powder
1 pound raw cashews
2 tablespoons seasoned salt

In a large saucepan, boil the water and stir in the salt, ginger, chili peppers, and curry powder. Cover, reduce heat to a simmer, and cook for 10 minutes. Add the nuts and bring to a second boil. Cover, reduce heat, and simmer for 10 minutes more.

Meanwhile, preheat the oven to 200 degrees.

Drain and dry the nuts with paper towels. Discard the chili peppers and ginger slices. Place the nuts on an ungreased baking sheet. Bake for 2 hours, stirring occasionally.

After removing the nuts from the oven, sprinkle with the seasoned salt and serve.

Makes 1 pound   PREPARATION TIME: 45 minutes
                                   BAKING TIME: 2 hours

PAKORAS

Introduce your family and friends to Indian cuisine with pakoras, a finger food that fits right in at picnics, parties, and potlucks.

2   cups chickpea flour
1   teaspoon salt
¼   teaspoon ground cumin
¼   teaspoon oregano seeds
¼   teaspoon paprika
⅛   teaspoon cayenne pepper
1   large potato, peeled and thinly cut
¼   cup vegetable oil
1   large onion, sliced and separated into rings

Combine the chickpea flour, salt, cumin, oregano seeds, paprika, and cayenne pepper with enough water to make a thick, cakelike batter. Set aside.

Boil the potato slices until almost tender. Drain on a paper towel to remove excess water.

Heat the oil in a skillet over medium-high heat. Dip the onion rings and potato slices into the batter. Coat the vegetables and fry in the oil until cooked thoroughly. Drain the excess oil on a paper towel, then serve immediately.

Makes 25 to 30 pakoras   PREPARATION TIME: 45 minutes

Variation: This recipe works well substituting any of your favorite vegetables.

BREADED ZUCCHINI STICKS WITH HORSERADISH DIP

Make plenty and watch 'em disappear!

1 cup unbleached all-purpose flour
Salt and pepper to taste
2 teaspoons garlic powder
4 medium zucchini, cut in half and sliced lengthwise
2 tablespoons olive oil

DIP

1   cup Eggless Mayonnaise (p. 85)
3–4 tablespoons prepared horseradish
Salt to taste

Combine the flour, salt, pepper, and garlic powder. Dip the zucchini sticks in the flour mixture and coat well.

In a large skillet, heat the olive oil over medium heat. Sauté the zucchini for about 5 minutes, then place zucchini on a paper towel to soak up any excess oil.

For the dip, combine the mayonnaise, horseradish, and salt. Arrange the zucchini sticks on a platter. Pour the horseradish dip into a small dip bowl and serve with the zucchini.

Serves 6 to 8   PREPARATION TIME: 25 minutes

COLD APPETIZERS

ENTREMES DE AGUACATE Y PAPAYA

This beautiful array of creamy avocado, sweet papaya, and tart lime creates a taste sensation that will have you dreaming of sunny days in the Caribbean.

1 ripe avocado, pitted, peeled, and sliced
1 ripe papaya, seeded, peeled, and sliced
Juice of 1 lime

Alternate the slices of avocado and papaya on a small serving dish. Sprinkle with the fresh lime juice. Serve immediately at room temperature.

Serves 4 to 6   PREPARATION TIME: 15 minutes

STUFFED CELERY

Jazz up that array of crudités with a Thai favorite. A deceptively simple treat that's great on sliced bananas, too.

⅔ cup peanut butter (crunchy or creamy)
3 teaspoons soy milk
3 teaspoons soy sauce or tamari
¼ teaspoon ground ginger
¼ cup toasted sesame seeds
Celery stalks

In a small bowl, cream together the first 5 ingredients in the order given. Stuff the celery stalks and cut to desired size.

Makes about 1 cup of filling   PREPARATION TIME: 10 minutes

BABA GHANOUSH

Enjoy the wonderful flavor of eggplant in this easy recipe from the Middle East. The mixture is good in a pita pocket or on crackers.

1 **large eggplant**
2 **cloves garlic**
3 **tablespoons tahini**
3 **tablespoons lemon juice**
½ **teaspoon salt**

Preheat the oven to 350 degrees.

Wash the eggplant and prick it in several places with a fork. Place on a baking sheet and bake until soft and beginning to collapse, about 45 minutes. Remove the eggplant from the oven and allow to cool.

After eggplant has cooled enough to handle, remove the skin and the seeds. In a blender or food processor, combine the eggplant pulp with the remaining ingredients and blend until smooth.

Refrigerate up to 1 day before serving, if desired, but it is also good at room temperature. Serve with pita bread or pita chips.

Makes 2 cups   PREPARATION TIME: 20 minutes
     BAKING TIME: 45 minutes

SALSA

Zesty salsa with a south-of-the-border taste—a favorite for chip dipping.

1   28-ounce can peeled tomatoes, drained and chopped
1   8-ounce can chopped green chilies, drained and chopped
1   6-ounce can pitted black olives, drained and chopped
8   green onions, chopped
¼   cup distilled white vinegar
¼   cup olive oil
2   teaspoons garlic salt

Mix all the ingredients in a bowl and chill. Stir before serving with corn tortilla chips.

Serves 6   PREPARATION TIME: 15 minutes

MOM'S BEST GUACAMOLE

Guacamole is by now an all-American treat, but the taste is strictly south of the border! Served with crisp tortilla chips, this appetizer turns any gathering into a party.

3   ripe avocados
1   small onion, minced
2   small tomatoes, chopped
Juice of 1 lemon
½   clove garlic, minced
¼   teaspoon salt or to taste
½   teaspoon pepper or to taste
¼–½   teaspoon chili powder
¼–½   teaspoon ground cumin

Gently peel and core the avocados, then mash. Add the onion, tomatoes, lemon juice, and spices and stir gently. Cover tightly with plastic wrap (push the wrap down onto the mixture so its surface does not brown). Refrigerate 1 hour or so before serving.

Serves 6 to 8   PREPARATION TIME: 15 minutes

CHILLING TIME: 1 hour

EGGPLANT RELISH

This exotic eggplant spread is an ideal addition to your tray of hors d'oeuvres.

2 large eggplants
1 large clove garlic, crushed
2 ripe tomatoes, seeded and chopped
2 tablespoons olive oil
2 teaspoons lemon juice
2 teaspoons chopped fresh basil
2 teaspoons chopped fresh parsley
Salt and pepper to taste

Preheat the oven to 350 degrees.

Wash the eggplant and prick it in several places with a fork. Place the eggplant on a baking sheet and bake until soft and beginning to collapse, about 45 minutes. Remove the eggplant from the oven and let cool.

Cut the eggplant in half and remove and discard the skin and seeds. Chop the pulp and transfer to a large bowl. Stir in the remaining ingredients, mix well, and serve at room temperature or chilled.

Serves 4 to 5   PREPARATION TIME: 10 minutes

BAKING TIME: 45 minutes

ONION DIP

This easy dip will become one of your staples.

1   **pound soft tofu**
2   **tablespoons lemon juice**
2   **teaspoons sugar**
½   **teaspoon soy sauce or tamari**
1   **package vegan dry onion soup mix (see Glossary of Ingredients)**

In a blender or food processor, combine the tofu, lemon juice, sugar, and soy sauce or tamari and blend until very smooth. Pour the mixture into a mixing bowl and stir in the soup mix. Stir well and refrigerate for 4 hours.

Serve with chips or raw vegetables.

Makes 3 cups   PREPARATION TIME: 15 minutes
                            CHILLING TIME: 4 hours

MARINATED MUSHROOMS

An elegant addition to your tray of hors d'oeuvres.

1   **cup water**
½   **cup olive oil**
½   **cup lemon juice or distilled white vinegar**
1   **teaspoon dried thyme**
1   **teaspoon dried tarragon**
1   **teaspoon salt**
½   **teaspoon peppercorns**
1   **pound fresh mushrooms, washed and patted dry**

In a medium saucepan, combine the water, oil, lemon juice, thyme, tarragon, salt, and peppercorns. Simmer, uncovered, for 5 minutes. Add the mushrooms, boil for 1 minute, and cool, uncovered.

Refrigerate overnight. Remove the mushrooms from the refrigerator about 30 minutes before serving and mix well. Drain the mushrooms, spear each with a toothpick, and serve.

Serves 4 to 6   PREPARATION TIME: 15 minutes
                                   CHILLING TIME: 8 hours

6 | SOUPS

"To my mind the life of a lamb is no less precious than that of a human being. I should be unwilling to take the life of a lamb for the sake of the human body."

—MAHATMA GANDHI

Some like it hot—but some like it not. That's why our soup recipes cover all temperatures and all seasons. This chapter offers a range of easy, healthful soups to suit everyone's mood and appetite. And the versatile vegetable broth gives you a base for creating your own wonderful soups and main dishes.

VEGETABLE BROTH

As is, this versatile soup is a warming side dish; it also makes a healthful, aromatic base for heartier soups, stews, and sauces.

½ teaspoon dried parsley
¼ teaspoon dried thyme
½ teaspoon black pepper
1 dried bay leaf
2 large carrots, sliced
2 stalks celery, sliced
2 medium white onions, thinly sliced
2 large white or red potatoes, quartered
1 large clove garlic
½ teaspoon salt

Put the prepared vegetables and herbs in a large pot and add water to cover. Bring the vegetables to a boil, uncovered. Lower the heat, cover, and simmer for 1½ hours.

Strain through a colander for a thin broth or stock. For a richer broth, puree the mixture in a blender.

Makes about 2 quarts   PREPARATION TIME: 20 minutes
                                  COOKING TIME: 1½ hours

VEGETABLE CHOWDER

For a rich summer vegetable soup supreme, look no further than this colorful chowder.

¼ cup margarine or water
1 cup chopped onions
1 cup chopped celery
½ cup plus 2 tablespoons unbleached all-purpose flour
4 cups Vegetable Broth (p. 52)
2 cups broccoli florets
1 cup sliced carrots
1 cup sliced zucchini
1 cup diced tomatoes
2 cups liquid nondairy creamer
2 cups soy milk
1 tablespoon salt or to taste
1 teaspoon pepper
1 tablespoon fresh thyme leaves

In a large saucepan over medium heat, heat the margarine or water. Add the onions and celery and cook until the onions are transparent, about 6 minutes. Stir in the flour and cook, stirring constantly, for 2 minutes; set aside.

In a large saucepan, bring the vegetable broth to a boil over high heat. Add the broccoli and carrots, lower the heat to medium, and cook for 3 minutes. Add the zucchini and tomatoes, and continue to cook for another 3 minutes, or until the vegetables are tender but crisp. Strain the vegetable stock into the onion-flour mixture and reserve the vegetables.

Over medium heat, cook the stock until it begins to thicken, stirring constantly. Add the vegetables, nondairy creamer, soy milk, salt, pepper, and thyme. Simmer until thoroughly heated.

Serve immediately.

Serves 6 to 8   PREPARATION TIME: 1 hour

CREAM OF ASPARAGUS SOUP

They will *want seconds.*

2½ cups Vegetable Broth (p. 52) or water
1   pound fresh asparagus, cut into ½-inch pieces
1   large potato, thinly sliced
½   medium onion, chopped
½   cup chopped celery
2   tablespoons unbleached all-purpose flour
2   cups soy milk
¼   teaspoon salt
¼   teaspoon pepper
¼   teaspoon dried tarragon

In a large saucepan over medium heat, bring the broth to a boil. Add the asparagus, potato, onion, and celery, then reduce the heat and cook for 25 to 30 minutes.

Pour the soup mixture into a food processor along with the flour and puree until smooth. Return the soup to the saucepan, add the remaining ingredients, and simmer until the soup begins to thicken and is heated through.

Serve immediately.

Serves 6   PREPARATION TIME: 15–40 minutes
                          CHILLING TIME: 2 hours

CREAM OF CARROT SOUP

A thermos filled with hot Cream of Carrot Soup is the ideal take-me-along for a day of snow-filled fun.

2 tablespoons margarine (¼ stick) or water
1 medium onion, chopped
12 medium carrots, sliced
1 medium potato, peeled and diced
4 cups Vegetable Broth (p. 52)
½ cup soy milk
Salt and pepper to taste
Dash of grated nutmeg
¼ teaspoon ground ginger
¼ teaspoon dried rosemary
1 tablespoon orange juice

Heat the margarine or water in a large saucepan. Cook the onion for 5 minutes over low heat, or until soft. Add the carrots and potato, cover, and simmer for 5 to 10 minutes. Add the broth, cover, and simmer about 20 minutes, or until the vegetables are tender.

Pour the soup through a sieve or colander, reserving the stock for later. Puree the vegetables in a blender or food processor and return them to the saucepan. Add the soy milk, then gradually add the reserved stock until the soup reaches the desired consistency.

Flavor with the remaining ingredients. Reheat slowly and serve.

Serves 6   PREPARATION TIME: 45 minutes

GREAT GAZPACHO

This soup is as pleasing to the nose and eyes as it is to the taste buds—and to the chef, who will find it a breeze to prepare.

3 cups vegetable or tomato juice
1 medium onion, minced
2 medium tomatoes, diced
1 green bell pepper, minced
1 clove garlic, crushed
1 medium cucumber, diced
2 tablespoons lemon juice
2 tablespoons red wine vinegar
1 teaspoon dried tarragon
1 teaspoon minced fresh basil
Pinch of ground cumin
Dash of hot sauce
2 tablespoons olive oil
Salt and pepper to taste

Combine all the ingredients and chill for 2 hours.

Hint: Out of time? Forget all the mincing and chopping. Cube the vegetables, then throw all of the ingredients into a blender or food processor and blend slowly until the vegetables are chunky and the soup is well blended.

Serves 6   PREPARATION TIME: 15–40 minutes
                              CHILLING TIME: 2 hours

SUMMERY CUKE SOUP

For those days when the mercury creeps up into the 90s and you're looking for a lighter meal.

2   **teaspoons vegetable oil**
5   **cucumbers, peeled, seeded, and chopped**
3   **cloves garlic**
2   **medium onions, chopped**
2½ **cups Vegetable Broth (p. 52)**
¼   **cup chopped fresh dill**
Pepper to taste
1   **cup soy milk**

In a large saucepan, heat the oil over medium heat and sauté the cucumbers, garlic, and onions until onions are transparent, about 6 minutes. Add the broth and simmer until the cucumber is soft, about 15 to 20 minutes.

Remove the soup from the heat and transfer to a blender or food processor and blend until smooth. While the mixture is still warm, stir in the dill and season with pepper. Chill. Stir in the soy milk just before serving.

Serves 6   PREPARATION TIME: 45 minutes
                                              CHILLING TIME: 2 hours

WATERCRESS SOUP

It takes a bit of time to make this flavorful soup with this underused summer green, but it is well worth the extra effort.

1 tablespoon margarine or water
2 medium onions, chopped
1 clove garlic, minced
2 medium potatoes, quartered and peeled
2 large bunches watercress, chopped
3 cups Vegetable Broth (p. 52)
2 cups soy milk
Salt and pepper to taste

Heat the margarine or water in a large saucepan over medium heat and lightly cook the onions and garlic for 3 minutes. Add the potatoes, watercress, and broth and simmer, covered, for 15 minutes or until the potatoes are tender.

Transfer the soup to a blender or food processor and puree the soup until smooth. Pour the mixture back into the saucepan and add the soy milk, salt, and pepper. Cook over low heat until the soup is heated through, then serve.

Serves 6 to 8   PREPARATION TIME: 1 hour

LINDA McCARTNEY'S AVOCADO AND GREEN CHILI SOUP

Knock their socks off with this powerhouse soup—great by itself or with a salad and toasted pita bread chips.

Adapted with permission from Linda McCartney's Home Cooking *by Linda McCartney and Peter Cox © 1989 by MPL Communications Ltd., by permission of Little, Brown and Company.*

2 ripe avocados
3 cups soy milk
1 4-ounce can or jar green chilies
1 medium onion, chopped
Salt and pepper to taste
2 tablespoons lemon juice
2 tablespoons dry sherry
Chopped chilies or fresh parsley, for garnish

Cut the avocados in half and remove the pits. Scoop out the avocado pulp and puree in a blender. Add the remaining ingredients except garnish to the blender and puree until evenly smooth. Pour the mixture into a serving bowl, garnish, and serve immediately.

Serves 4 to 6   PREPARATION TIME: 10 minutes

TOMATO RICE SOUP

An old favorite made simply delicious. Serve it with a salad for a light lunch or with sandwiches for a hearty meal.

1 tablespoon vegetable oil
2 tablespoons unbleached all-purpose flour
4 cups canned tomato sauce
1 small onion
2 cups cooked rice

Heat the oil in a large saucepan and brown the flour in the oil. Add the tomato sauce and the onion. Cook over low heat for 15 minutes.

Add the rice to the pan and continue cooking until the soup is thoroughly heated. Remove the onion (you can save it for making vegetable stock or throw it in the compost) and serve.

Serves 4   PREPARATION TIME: 15 minutes

GOBLIN SOUP

Frightfully good! This satisfying autumn soup will warm you to the bones.

1   tablespoon margarine or water
1   medium onion, chopped
1   16-ounce can pumpkin puree
1⅓ cups water
3   cups soy milk
½   teaspoon grated nutmeg
½   teaspoon sugar
Pepper to taste
Croutons

In a large saucepan over medium heat, heat the margarine or water and cook the onion until tender, stirring often, about 5 minutes. Stir in the pumpkin, water, soy milk, nutmeg, sugar, and pepper. Cook over medium heat until just boiling, stirring constantly. Garnish with croutons.

Serves 6   PREPARATION TIME: 15 minutes

CURRIED SPLIT PEA AND POTATO SOUP

Serve this soup at a large gathering, or save it in the fridge for fast, easy meals later in the week. So thick and hearty, it's the perfect answer on even your hungriest days.

16 ounces green split peas, dried
10 cups water
1 large onion, chopped
1 teaspoon garlic powder
1 teaspoon dried oregano
1 teaspoon curry powder
½ teaspoon pepper
½ teaspoon salt
1 bay leaf
2 large carrots, peeled and chopped
3 medium potatoes, peeled and chopped
2 stalks celery, chopped

In a large saucepan, combine the split peas, water, onion, and spices. Simmer, uncovered, for 1 hour. Stir in the carrots, potatoes, and celery. Simmer, covered, stirring occasionally, for an additional 45 minutes or until the soup reaches desired thickness. Remove bay leaf. Puree in a blender or food processor. Reheat before serving.

Serves 10   PREPARATION TIME: 15 minutes
                               COOKING TIME: 1¾ hours

CORN CHOWDER

A hearty chowder that's sure to warm a winter chill.

5   medium potatoes, chopped
3   cups water or Vegetable Broth (p. 52)
2   teaspoons vegetable oil or water
1   medium onion, chopped
2   stalks celery, diced
2   medium carrots, chopped
1   red bell pepper, diced
1   teaspoon salt
1   teaspoon black pepper
1   cup soy milk
2½   cups frozen corn kernels

In a medium saucepan, boil the potatoes in the water or broth for 20 minutes.

While the potatoes are cooking, heat the oil or water in a medium frying pan over medium heat. Add the onion, celery, carrots, red bell pepper, salt, and pepper. Cook until just tender, about 5 to 7 minutes.

When the potatoes are soft, remove them from the saucepan and reserve the stock. Blend the potatoes with the soy milk in a blender or food processor until smooth.

Return the soup to the saucepan and stir in the corn, onion mixture, and enough of the reserved stock to achieve a creamy thick consistency. Heat thoroughly before serving.

Serves 6   PREPARATION TIME: 45 minutes

FRENCH ONION SOUP

A classic that's so easy and inexpensive, you'll find yourself making it time and time again.

2   tablespoons vegetable oil or water
2–3 large onions, sliced
¼   cup unbleached all-purpose flour
4   cups water
¼   cup soy sauce or tamari
4   slices French bread, toasted; or croutons

Heat the oil or water in a large saucepan over medium heat. Add the onions and cook for 2 minutes. Add the flour and stir until the onions are well coated. Add the water and soy sauce or tamari, and stir well. Bring the soup to a boil, then turn heat to low and simmer, covered, until the onions are tender. Add more water if soup becomes too thick.

Serve in individual bowls topped with the French bread or croutons.

Serves 4   PREPARATION TIME: 10 minutes

LENTIL SOUP

This hearty and heart-warming soup is comfort food at its best.

1   teaspoon vegetable oil
1   medium onion, sliced
1   medium carrot, sliced
4   cups hot Vegetable Broth (p. 52)
1   cup lentils
¼   teaspoon pepper
¼   teaspoon dried thyme
2   bay leaves
Salt to taste
1   tablespoon lemon juice

Heat the oil in a large pot over medium heat, then sauté the onion and carrot for about 5 minutes or until tender. Add the broth, lentils, pepper, thyme, bay leaves, and salt. Cover and simmer until lentils are tender, about 40 to 50 minutes. Stir in the lemon juice and extra salt to taste.

Serves 6 to 8   PREPARATION TIME: 10 minutes
                                   COOKING TIME: 50 minutes

CREAM OF BROCCOLI SOUP

Serve with a selection of good breads for a satisfying supper.

1	**pound broccoli**
1	**medium onion, quartered**
1	**clove garlic**
2	**cups Vegetable Broth (p. 52) or water**
¼	**cup unbleached all-purpose flour**
2½	**cups soy milk**
2	**tablespoons soy sauce or tamari**
2	**teaspoons basil**

Salt and pepper to taste

Cut the broccoli into florets and slice about one-fourth of the top of each stem. Reserve 1 cup of florets.

Put the broccoli, onion, garlic, and broth or water in a large saucepan. Bring to a boil, then reduce the heat to medium and cook until the vegetables are tender, about 15 minutes.

Put all the ingredients into a food processor and add the flour. Process until smooth. Return the soup to the saucepan; add the remaining ingredients and the florets. Cook over medium heat until the soup thickens and is heated through.

Season to taste with the salt and pepper and serve.

Serves 6 to 8   PREPARATION TIME: 30 minutes

NAVY BEAN SOUP

Be sure to make enough for seconds all around.

Reprinted with permission from The Peaceful Palate: Fine Vegetarian Cuisine *by Jennifer Raymond.*

1	**pound navy beans (2 cups)**
8	**cups water**
1	**medium onion, chopped**
1	**clove garlic, minced**
1	**cup sliced carrots**
1	**cup sliced celery**
1	**large potato, scrubbed and diced**
1	**bay leaf**
½	**cup tomato sauce**
¼	**teaspoon dried thyme**
⅛	**teaspoon black pepper**
1	**tablespoon chopped fresh parsley**
1–1½	**teaspoons salt**

Wash the beans and soak overnight in about 4 cups of water. Pour off the soaking water and place the beans in a kettle or large saucepan with the water, onion, garlic, carrots, celery, potato, and bay leaf.

Bring the mixture to a simmer, and cook until the beans are tender, about 1½ hours. Remove bay leaf.

Puree the soup in a blender in several small batches. Be sure to start on low speed and hold the lid on tightly. Stir in the tomato sauce and seasonings. Add salt to taste.

Serves 8 to 10   PREPARATION TIME: 30 minutes
                                    SOAKING TIME: 8 hours
                                    COOKING TIME: 1½ hours

MUNG DAHL SOUP

Impress your friends and family with a taste of traditional Indian cuisine.

1   **cup split husked mung dahl beans or yellow split peas**
2   **cups water**
1   **teaspoon turmeric**
¼   **teaspoon cayenne pepper**
1   **teaspoon salt**
2   **tablespoons (¼ stick) margarine**
1   **large onion, cut into paper-thin slivers**
1   **teaspoon cumin seeds**
1   **whole clove**

Pick over the beans or peas and discard any discolored ones or any small stones. Wash the beans in a colander under cold running water. Pour the beans into a heavy 2- to 3-quart saucepan. Add the water, turmeric, cayenne pepper, and salt and bring to a boil over high heat. Reduce the heat to low and cover partly. Simmer for 30 minutes.

Meanwhile, in a medium frying pan over high heat, melt the margarine, then add the onion, cumin seeds, and clove and reduce the heat to medium. Sauté until the onion is transparent and soft, about 6 minutes.

Once the beans have cooked through, add the onion mixture and simmer for 1 to 2 more minutes. Serve immediately.

Serves 4 to 6

PREPARATION TIME: 30 minutes
COOKING TIME: 30 minutes

7 | SALADS AND DRESSINGS

"I became a vegetarian when I was 22 or 23. It happened when I was in Paris and I was walking through the market district called Halles. There was just row after row of carcasses...and that did it for me. I could never eat meat after that."

—CANDICE BERGEN

Ah, salads. It seems the longer you're a vegetarian, the greater your craving grows for these healthful, delicious dishes, and the more they become a staple in your diet.

We've collected some very special salads, with out-of-the-ordinary combinations like spinach and nuts or cold brown rice and vegetables. We also give you a selection of savory salad dressings like a raspberry vinaigrette and a tropical citrus dressing that can spruce up a plain green salad.

Here are salads that can make the meal or play a side role. Try a pasta salad for a main dish, or make a meal out of a large tossed salad, soup, and French bread. The possibilities and variations of salads are limited only by your imagination!

SALADS

MARINATED PEA SALAD

Terrific served on a lovely leaf of lettuce, or as a substantial addition to a salad buffet.

¾ **cup distilled white vinegar**
¾ **cup sugar**
1   **tablespoon water**
1   **15- to 17-ounce can petite peas, drained**
1   **16-ounce can corn kernels, drained**
1   **cup chopped celery**
1   **cup chopped onions**

Combine the vinegar, sugar, and water in a small saucepan. Bring to a boil over medium heat. Boil for 5 minutes, then remove from the heat and cool completely.

In a medium bowl, combine the remaining ingredients. Pour the cooled vinegar mixture over the vegetables and chill 4 hours or overnight.

Serves 4 to 6

PREPARATION TIME: 20 minutes
CHILLING TIME: 4 hours or overnight

TABOULEH

Add a scoop of tabouleh on the side to make a snappy salad. (Grains make great salads—you won't even realize it's good for you!) Or serve it with Hummus (p. 26), Baba Ghanoush (p. 45), and warm pita bread for a Middle Eastern feast.

4   cups water
¾   cup bulgur wheat
2   medium tomatoes, seeded and diced
4   tablespoons finely minced onion
2   cups finely chopped fresh parsley
3   tablespoons lemon juice
1   teaspoon salt
2   tablespoons olive oil

Boil the water, pour it over the bulgur, and let stand for 45 minutes. When bulgur has swollen, drain the excess water, then squeeze by handfuls to remove any additional. In a bowl, combine with the remaining ingredients and mix well. Adjust seasonings as needed.

Serves 6   PREPARATION TIME: 15 minutes
                              SOAKING TIME: 45 minutes

RICE SALAD

This colorful and festive dish, perfect for an outdoor gathering with family or friends, will have everyone asking, "Who made the salad?"

2   cups cooked rice
2   cups corn kernels, canned or frozen
2   green bell peppers, diced
1½   cups cooked kidney beans
1   small onion, chopped
6   tablespoons distilled white vinegar
3   tablespoons vegetable oil
2   teaspoons soy sauce or tamari
2   teaspoons prepared mustard
1   teaspoon prepared horseradish

Mix the rice, corn, peppers, kidney beans, and onion in a bowl. Combine the vinegar, oil, tamari, mustard, and horseradish in a small bowl and pour over the other ingredients. Toss well.

Serves 4   PREPARATION TIME: 10 minutes

PEANUTTY SALAD

You can't judge a book by its cover and you can't judge a salad by its colors. This modest-looking salad surprises with a delicious punch of peanutty flavor.

1   cup prepared Italian dressing or Italian Herb Dressing (p. 87)
¼   cup peanut butter (creamy or chunky)
1   head iceberg, leaf, and/or romaine lettuces, torn into bite-size
     pieces

Croutons
Sunflower seeds or chopped peanuts
Finely chopped green onions (optional)

In a small bowl, gradually blend the dressing into the peanut butter using a wire whisk. Toss the lettuce, croutons, sunflower seeds or peanuts, and green onions in a bowl. Place in individual salad bowls and top with peanut butter dressing. (Makes 1¼ cups dressing.)

Serves 4 to 5   PREPARATION TIME: 10 minutes

RED POTATO SALAD

So inexpensive and simple to make you might feel guilty. Don't—no one will guess!

12–15 large unpeeled red potatoes, cut into bite-size wedges
4   stalks celery, sliced
1   large green bell pepper, cut into small squares
6   green onions, chopped
2   cups prepared Italian dressing or Italian Herb Dressing (p. 87)
Garlic salt and pepper to taste

Boil the potatoes for about 15 minutes or until tender. In a large bowl, mix all the ingredients while the potatoes are still hot. Chill for 2 to 3 hours.

Serves 6   PREPARATION TIME: 20 minutes
                            CHILLING TIME: 2–3 hours

CHICKPEA SALAD

A delightful summer dish that takes just minutes to make, Chickpea Salad is sure to be a hit at your picnic.

1   16-ounce can chickpeas, drained
3   stalks celery, diced
¾   cup Eggless Mayonnaise (p. 85)
2   tablespoons lemon juice
1   clove garlic, minced
1   teaspoon minced fresh parsley
1   tablespoon chopped onion
Salt and pepper to taste

Mix the chickpeas and celery. Add the remaining ingredients and season to taste. Serve in pita pockets or as an individual salad.

Serves 4   PREPARATION TIME: 15 minutes

CREAMY COLESLAW

You'll get carried away by the great caraway flavor in this simple-to-make coleslaw.

1½ cups shredded green cabbage
1   medium carrot, grated
½   small onion, finely chopped
2   tablespoons lemon juice
¾   cup Eggless Mayonnaise (p. 85)
1   tablespoon caraway seeds
Salt and pepper to taste

Combine all the ingredients in a large salad bowl. Sprinkle with the salt and pepper and serve.

Serves 3 to 4   PREPARATION TIME: 20 minutes

CREAMY PASTA SALAD

This is no ordinary pasta salad; it's got (artichoke) heart and soul, and will add zest to any luncheon.

¼ **cup Eggless Mayonnaise (p. 85)**
2 **tablespoons lemon juice**
2 **cups cooked noodles (elbow, rotini, or small shells)**
4 **green onions, chopped**
1 **6-ounce jar artichoke hearts, drained and sliced**
1½ **tablespoons fresh or dried basil**
½ **teaspoon salt**

Stir the eggless mayonnaise and lemon juice into the noodles. Add the green onions, artichoke hearts, basil, and salt and mix well. If the salad is too dry, add more mayonnaise and/or lemon juice.

Serves 4   PREPARATION TIME: 25 minutes

JEANNE'S CREAMY POTATO SALAD

Hard-core deli shoppers will demand the recipe for this yummy potato salad!

6   medium potatoes, boiled
½   cup Eggless Mayonnaise (p. 85)
¼   cup distilled white vinegar
1   large onion, chopped
1   cup chopped celery
Salt and pepper to taste
Paprika (optional)

Cut the potatoes into cubes. Combine all the ingredients in a bowl and season to taste. Sprinkle paprika on top, if desired.

Serves 4 to 6   PREPARATION TIME: 15 minutes

JOJO'S NUTTY SLAW

Get a double crunch from your coleslaw—first from fresh cabbage and then from the seeds or nuts you add to it—a snappy twist on an old favorite!

½   head green cabbage, shredded
½   head red cabbage, shredded
½   cup roasted sunflower seeds or chopped nuts
½   cup Eggless Mayonnaise (p. 85)
¼   cup lemon juice
Salt and pepper to taste

Place all the ingredients in a large mixing bowl. Stir well. Chill, then serve.

Serves 8 to 12   PREPARATION TIME: 20 minutes
                                    CHILLING TIME: 30 minutes

ORIENTAL BROWN RICE SALAD

A light, flavorful salad that's great for the lazy days of summer.

4   cups cold cooked brown rice
¼   cup peanut oil
1   teaspoon salt
½   teaspoon pepper
1   teaspoon sugar
1   teaspoon roasted sesame oil
1   medium carrot, peeled and diced
½   cup chopped snow peas
½   cup frozen corn kernels
¼   cup rice vinegar
1   stalk celery, diced
½   red bell pepper, diced
3   green onions, chopped
2   tablespoons chopped fresh parsley

Place the rice in a large mixing bowl.

In a small mixing bowl, combine the peanut oil, salt, pepper, sugar, and sesame oil. Stir until the sugar dissolves, then pour over the rice, toss, and set aside.

Steam the carrot, snow peas, and corn in or over a small amount of boiling water for 1 minute. Rinse the vegetables in cold water. Drain and stir the vegetables into the rice. Add the remaining ingredients and toss to mix well. Refrigerate for 1 to 2 hours and serve cold.

Serves 4 to 6   PREPARATION TIME: 25 minutes

                                   CHILLING TIME: 1–2 hours

THREE BEAN SALAD

There's no skimping with this yummy side-dish salad. With plenty of each of three kinds of beans, plus crunchy celery and green pepper, it's a meal in itself!

¾   **cup sugar**
⅓   **cup vegetable oil**
⅔   **cup distilled white vinegar**
1   **16-ounce can green beans**
1   **16-ounce can garbanzo beans**
1   **16-ounce can red kidney beans**
1   **green bell pepper, sliced**
1½ **cups chopped celery**
1   **green onion, chopped**

Bring the sugar, oil, and vinegar to a boil in a saucepan. Let cool.

Meanwhile, drain the beans and combine in a large bowl. Add the green pepper, celery, and green onion. Pour the dressing over the beans and vegetables. Toss gently and let marinate overnight in the fridge.

Serves 8 to 10   PREPARATION TIME: 20 minutes

                                   MARINATING TIME: 8 hours

FRESH FRUIT SALAD WITH POPPY SEED DRESSING

Fresh fruit salads are one of summer's treasures. This special poppy seed dressing enhances the sweet delight of luscious melons and berries.

½   cup unsweetened orange juice
⅓   cup unsweetened grapefruit juice
1½ tablespoons cornstarch
2   teaspoons vegetable oil
2   teaspoons sugar
1   teaspoon poppy seeds
Pulp of 1 honeydew melon, chopped
Pulp of 1 cantaloupe, chopped
2   nectarines, pitted and chopped
1   pint strawberries, sliced
½   cup blueberries

Combine the orange and grapefruit juices, cornstarch, oil, and sugar in a saucepan. Stir well until all lumps are dissolved. Cook over medium heat, stirring constantly, until thickened, about 5 minutes. Remove from the heat and add the poppy seeds. Stir thoroughly, cover, and chill.

Combine all the fruit in a large salad bowl and toss. Refrigerate until serving. Pour the dressing over the fruit right before serving.

Serves 6 to 8   PREPARATION TIME: 30 minutes

SPINACH AND CASHEW SALAD

Seems so basic and simple, you might not think it's apropos to serve Aunt Flo. Guess again. This salad gives meaning to the phrase "less is more."

1½ cups chopped raw spinach leaves
½   cup watercress
4   green onions, sliced
⅓   cup cashews
½   cup croutons
Your favorite vegan salad dressing

Combine the spinach, watercress, green onions, and cashews in a serving bowl. Spoon the dressing over the salad and toss. Eat immediately while crisp.

Serves 4   PREPARATION TIME: 15 minutes

SUMMER BEAN AND RICE SALAD

The perfect salad for those times when you're craving a light but filling meal.

2   cups cooked rice, cooled
1   cup canned black beans, drained
1   tablespoon chopped fresh parsley leaves
1   medium tomato, seeded and chopped
¼   cup Italian Herb Dressing (p. 87)
1   tablespoon lime juice
Lettuce

Combine the rice, black beans, parsley, and tomato in a large bowl. Pour the dressing and lime juice over the mixture; toss lightly. Arrange on a bed of lettuce.

Serves 4   PREPARATION TIME: 15 minutes

TOFU SALAD

A delicious salad that's also a great sandwich spread. Destined to become a lunchtime favorite.

¾ **pound soft tofu**
¾ **pound firm tofu**
½ **medium onion, chopped fine**
2 **medium carrots, finely chopped**
⅓ **cup nutritional yeast**
2 **teaspoons soy sauce or tamari**
1½ **teaspoons garlic powder**
1½ **teaspoons salt**
Dash of pepper
2 **tablespoons vegetable oil**
Dash of paprika
Red leaf lettuce
Tomato slices

Crumble tofu with a fork. Add the ingredients as listed, stirring in the oil last. Sprinkle with paprika. Serve on a bed of red leaf lettuce, surrounded by tomatoes.

Serves 6   PREPARATION TIME: 10 minutes

ITALIAN PASTA SALAD

Zesty Italian dressing enhances the flavor of chunky vegetables and pasta.

1½   cups shell pasta
2   cups broccoli florets
1   cup cauliflower florets
1   cup sliced fresh mushrooms
1   6-ounce can artichoke hearts, drained and chopped
½   cup chopped onion
1   cup Italian Herb Dressing (p. 87)
¾   cup sliced black olives
1   medium tomato, chopped
1   medium avocado, pitted, peeled, and chopped

Cook the pasta according to package directions. Drain and rinse with cold water. Drain well.

In a large salad bowl, combine the pasta, broccoli, cauliflower, mushrooms, artichoke hearts, and onion. Toss with the dressing. Cover and chill for 4 hours.

Before serving, toss the salad with the olives, tomato, and avocado.

Serves 6 to 8   PREPARATION TIME: 15 minutes
                                 CHILLING TIME: 4 hours

WALDORF SALAD

Adam's apples everywhere will be singing the praises of your salad!

4   tart medium red apples, cored and diced (do not peel)
½   cup finely chopped celery

⅓ cup coarsely chopped walnuts
Approximately ⅔ cup Eggless Mayonnaise (p. 85)
Salt to taste
Lettuce

Stir all the ingredients in a bowl, adding just enough mayonnaise for good consistency. Cover and chill 2 to 3 hours. Stir well and serve on a bed of lettuce leaves.

Serves 4   PREPARATION TIME: 20 minutes
                                   CHILLING TIME: 2–3 hours

DRESSINGS

CITRUS DRESSING

A thousand thank-you's! to the genius who created this bold and unusual combination, guaranteed to add a tangy twang to your salad greens.

¾ cup orange juice
6 tablespoons mustard
1 cup olive oil
Salt and pepper to taste
Mixed lettuce

In a blender, puree the orange juice, mustard, and olive oil. Season to taste. Serve over mixed fresh greens.

Makes 2 cups   PREPARATION TIME: 5–10 minutes

THOUSAND ISLAND DRESSING

Here's all of the zing of the original without the clobber of cholesterol.

1   **cup Eggless Mayonnaise (p. 85)**
⅓   **cup ketchup**
½   **teaspoon onion powder**
¼   **teaspoon salt**
⅛   **teaspoon garlic powder**
3   **tablespoons sweet pickle relish**
2   **tablespoons minced stuffed green olives**

Blend the ingredients thoroughly in a mixing bowl.

Makes about 2 cups   PREPARATION TIME: 10 minutes

TOFU SOUR CREAM

You'll find so many uses for this sour cream, it's a good thing it takes almost no time to whip up!

¼   **pound soft tofu, patted dry**
¼   **pound firm tofu, patted dry**
1   **tablespoon lemon juice**
1   **teaspoon soy sauce or tamari**

Put all the ingredients in a blender and blend until creamy.

Makes 1 cup   PREPARATION TIME: 15 minutes

EGGLESS MAYONNAISE

This mayonnaise tastes so much like the real thing you'd swear it has cholesterol, but since it doesn't, feel free to spread it around!

3   tablespoons lemon juice
½   cup soy milk
¼   teaspoon salt
¼   teaspoon paprika
¼   teaspoon prepared mustard
6   tablespoons vegetable oil

Put all the ingredients except the oil in a blender. Blend on the lowest speed. Gradually—literally one drop at a time—add the oil until the mixture starts to thicken. Continue blending until thickened and smooth. Transfer to a jar and store in the refrigerator.

Makes ¾ cup   PREPARATION TIME: 20 minutes

FRENCH DRESSING

Remember the 4-3-2-1 rule to fix this salad dressing in a jiffy, and use it to jazz up plate of crudités!

4   tablespoons vegetable oil
3   tablespoons ketchup
2   tablespoons apple cider vinegar
1   tablespoon sugar
¼   teaspoon garlic powder

Combine all the ingredients in a bottle or jar and shake until the dressing is thoroughly mixed.

Makes ½ cup   PREPARATION TIME: 5 minutes

DIJON VINAIGRETTE

So simple to make, Dijon Vinaigrette will become a staple for your vegetable salads.

¾   cup olive oil
⅓   cup red wine vinegar
2   garlic cloves, pressed
¼   teaspoon salt
1   tablespoon Dijon mustard
¼   teaspoon black pepper
1   teaspoon minced fresh parsley
2   teaspoons minced fresh basil
½–1 teaspoon sugar

Put all the ingredients in a jar with a tight lid and shake vigorously. Good with green salads. If refrigerated, it will keep indefinitely.

Makes 1¼ cups   PREPARATION TIME: 10 minutes

RASPBERRY VINAIGRETTE

Treat your taste buds to a bit a heaven.

1½ cups fresh raspberries
1   tablespoon sugar
¼   teaspoon dried thyme leaves
¼   teaspoon pepper
2   tablespoons distilled white vinegar
3   tablespoons water
1½ teaspoons vegetable oil
¼   teaspoon salt

Combine all the ingredients in a blender and blend until smooth. Strain to remove the seeds. Chill for 4 hours.

Makes 1 cup   PREPARATION TIME: 15 minutes
                                 CHILLING TIME: 4 hours

ITALIAN HERB DRESSING

If you want to jazz up a potato, rice, pasta, or green salad, try this flavorful Italian dressing—the most versatile dressing in the world.

2 **cloves garlic, minced**
1 **teaspoon dried tarragon**
1 **teaspoon dried marjoram**
1 **teaspoon dry mustard**
½ **teaspoon salt**
¼ **teaspoon pepper**
½ **cup olive oil**
2 **tablespoons red wine vinegar**

Combine all the ingredients in a jar with a tight lid. Shake the jar well and let stand for 1 hour at room temperature, then chill. Shake well before serving.

Makes ⅔ cup   PREPARATION TIME: 15 minutes
                                 CHILLING TIME: 30 minutes
                                 RESTING TIME: 1 hour

8 | BREADS AND MUFFINS

"Non-violence leads to the highest ethics, which is the goal of all evolution. Until we stop harming all other living beings, we are still savages."

—THOMAS EDISON

Many would agree that one of life's simplest joys is breaking bread with friends and family. Many newcomers to vegetarianism are pleasantly surprised when they realize that breads, biscuits, and muffins are a cinch to make without a drop of milk, egg, or other animal ingredient.

In the pages that follow you'll find all sorts of tempting recipes, from traditional favorites like corn muffins to new ideas such as a summer dill bread to delicious basics like baking powder biscuits.

YEAST BREADS

FRENCH BREAD

There's nothing like crusty warm French bread right out of the oven, and the best way to get that is to make it yourself. Here's our version of this centuries-old favorite.

1½ packages active dry yeast
1   tablespoon sugar
2   cups lukewarm water (see Note, p. 91)
1   tablespoon salt
About 6 cups unbleached all-purpose flour
3   tablespoons cornmeal
1   tablespoon soy milk mixed with 1 tablespoon water

In a large mixing bowl, dissolve the yeast and the sugar in the lukewarm water. Allow the yeast to grow for 5 minutes.

Mix the salt with the flour, then stir it into the yeast mixture, 1 cup at a time, until you have a stiff dough. (You may need less than 6 cups. If so, save the rest for kneading the dough.) Remove the dough to a lightly floured bread board or countertop and knead the dough until it is no longer sticky, adding more flour as necessary. This should take about 10 minutes.

Place the dough in a greased bowl and turn it so that the entire surface is coated. Cover the dough and let it rise in a warm place until doubled in bulk, about 1½ to 2 hours.

Punch down the dough. Turn it out onto the floured bread board or countertop and divide in two. Pat each half into a flat oblong. Roll the dough away from you to create two long cylindrical loaves.

Place the loaves on a baking sheet that has been sprinkled with cornmeal. With a knife, slash the tops of the loaves diagonally in three places, then brush with the soy milk and water mixture.

Place the dough in the cold oven, then set the temperature to 400 degrees. Bake for 35 minutes, or until well browned and hollow sounding when tapped with your knuckles.

Makes 2 loaves   PREPARATION TIME: 2½ hours
                                     BAKING TIME: 35 minutes

Note: The temperature of lukewarm water is 85 to 105 degrees. To test for the correct temperature, drop a few drops onto the inside of your wrist. If it is lukewarm the water will feel neither hot nor cold.

SUMMER DILL BREAD

Try heating a slice of this flavorful bread with margarine, and a little nutritional yeast sprinkled on top for a cheesy taste.

1   **package active dry yeast**
2   **tablespoons sugar**
1¼ **cups lukewarm water**
2   **cups unbleached all-purpose flour**
1   **cup whole wheat flour**
2   **tablespoons vegetable oil**
1½ **teaspoons grated lemon rind**
2   **tablespoons lemon juice**
¼   **teaspoon salt**
1½ **teaspoons dried dill**

In a large bowl, dissolve the yeast and 1 tablespoon of the sugar in the lukewarm water. (See note about lukewarm water, above.) Let the mixture stand for 5 minutes. In another large bowl, combine 1 cup of the all-purpose flour, ½ cup of the whole wheat flour, and the oil, lemon rind, lemon juice, salt, and dill.

Add the yeast mixture to the flour mixture and beat at medium speed with an electric mixer for 2 minutes, scraping the sides of the bowl frequently. Add the remaining flour and sugar and stir well. Cover and let rise in a warm place for 40 minutes or until doubled in bulk.

Stir or punch the dough down. Grease an 8 ½ × 4 ½-inch loaf pan. Pour the batter into the pan, smooth the top of the batter with floured hands, and pat it into a loaf shape. Cover the dough again and let it rise 40 minutes or until doubled in bulk.

Preheat the oven to 375 degrees. Bake for 35 to 40 minutes or until the loaf sounds hollow when tapped. Remove the bread from the pan, and let cool on a wire rack.

Makes 1 loaf   PREPARATION TIME: 2 hours
                                    BAKING TIME: 40 minutes

HERB AND ONION BREAD

Who would want store-bought bread when there's fresh, homemade herb bread around? Great plain or with a dollop of softened margarine, this savory bread will disappear fast.

½   cup soy milk
1½   tablespoons sugar
1   teaspoon salt
1   tablespoon margarine
1   package active dry yeast
½   cup lukewarm water
2¼   cups unbleached all-purpose or whole wheat flour
½   small onion, minced

½   **teaspoon dried dill**
1   **teaspoon crushed dried rosemary**

Heat the soy milk until tiny bubbles form around the edge of the pan, and stir in the sugar, salt, and margarine; cool to lukewarm (see note about lukewarm temperature on page 91). In a large bowl, dissolve the yeast in the lukewarm water. Add the cooled soy milk mixture, flour, minced onion, and herbs, and stir well with a wooden spoon. When the dough is smooth, cover the bowl with a towel and let the dough rise in a warm place until triple in bulk, about 45 minutes.

Preheat the oven to 350 degrees. Stir the dough down and beat vigorously for a few minutes, then turn into a greased 8½ × 4½-inch bread pan. Let stand in a warm place about 10 minutes before baking for 1 hour.

Makes 1 loaf   PREPARATION TIME: 90 minutes
                                  BAKING TIME: 1 hour

QUICK BREADS

BAKING POWDER BISCUITS

Light and flaky biscuits are ideal for breakfast or with soups, chili, or salads.

2   **cups unbleached all-purpose flour**
1   **tablespoon baking powder**
½   **teaspoon salt**
4   **tablespoons (½ stick) margarine**
¾   **cup soy milk**

Preheat the oven to 450 degrees.

Put all the dry ingredients into a bowl. Using a pastry cutter or a fork, blend the margarine into the dry ingredients until the mixture breaks down into fine particles. Add the soy milk and stir until the particles cling together. Turn out onto a floured bread board or countertop and knead for 1 to 2 minutes or until the dough is smooth. Add more flour as needed if the dough is sticky.

With a rolling pin, roll the dough out to about a ½-inch thickness. Cut into rounds (a drinking glass works well), place on an ungreased cookie sheet, and bake for 12 to 15 minutes. Serve hot.

Makes 12 biscuits   PREPARATION TIME: 10 minutes
                                   BAKING TIME: 12–15 minutes

BANANA BREAD

In this easy recipe, the walnuts are optional, but the great flavor isn't!

⅓   **cup margarine**
½   **cup sugar**
2   **cups unbleached all-purpose flour**
1½   **teaspoons baking powder**
½   **teaspoon baking soda**
2   **ripe bananas, mashed**
½   **cup soy milk**
1   **teaspoon vanilla extract**
½   **cup chopped walnuts (optional)**

Preheat the oven to 350 degrees.

Cream the margarine and sugar, then stir in the flour, baking powder, and baking soda. Add the remaining ingredients and mix well. Pour into an oiled 8½ × 4½-inch bread pan and bake for 50 minutes.

Makes 1 loaf   PREPARATION TIME: 15 minutes
                                            BAKING TIME: 50 minutes

BEER BREAD

At last, a use for warm beer! For an intoxicatingly good bread, try this humble but slightly unorthodox recipe.

3   cups self-rising flour
3   tablespoons sugar
¼   teaspoon salt
1½ cups warm beer

Preheat the oven to 350 degrees.

In a large mixing bowl, combine the flour, sugar, and salt. Mix well. Add the beer and mix until blended. Pour into a well-greased 8½ × 4½-inch loaf pan and bake for 50 minutes, or until a toothpick inserted in the center comes out clean. Turn the warm bread out of the loaf pan and cool on a rack.

Makes 1 loaf   PREPARATION TIME: 15 minutes
                                            BAKING TIME: 50 minutes

QUICK RYE BREAD

Freshly baked crusty rye bread and an Avocado Reuben (p. 25)—a match made in heaven.

1   cup soy milk
1   tablespoon cider vinegar
1   tablespoon sugar
3   tablespoons molasses
1½ cups rye flour
¾   cup unbleached all-purpose flour
½   cup rolled oats
2   tablespoons caraway seeds
1½ teaspoons baking powder
½   teaspoon baking soda

Preheat the oven to 350 degrees.

In a small bowl, mix the soy milk, vinegar, sugar, and molasses. Set aside.

In a large bowl, combine the rye flour, all-purpose flour, oats, caraway seeds, baking powder, and baking soda. Add the soy milk mixture and stir well. Turn the dough onto a lightly floured bread board or countertop and knead until slightly sticky, 2 to 3 minutes (If the dough remains very sticky, knead in a little more flour.)

Shape the dough into a round and place it on a lightly oiled baking sheet. Bake until crusty and well browned, about 1 hour.

Serve warm.

Makes 1 loaf   PREPARATION TIME: 15 minutes
                                  BAKING TIME: 1 hour

ZUCCHINI BREAD

Sweet, warmed zucchini bread with a dollop of margarine is an irresistible treat.

2 cups grated zucchini (about 6 medium-sized)
Egg replacer equivalent of 3 eggs
1 cup oil
2 cups sugar
1 teaspoon vanilla extract
3 cups unbleached all-purpose flour
1 teaspoon salt
1 tablespoon baking soda
1 tablespoon ground cinnamon
2 teaspoons grated nutmeg
1 teaspoon baking powder

Preheat the oven to 350 degrees. Lightly oil 2 bread pans.

Stir together the zucchini, egg replacer, oil, sugar, and vanilla. Add the dry ingredients and stir well. Pour the batter into the prepared 8½ × 4½-inch pans and bake for 50 to 60 minutes.

Makes 2 loaves   PREPARATION TIME: 20 minutes
                                    BAKING TIME: 50–60 minutes

FRIED POTATO ROLLS

Great in the morning beside Smoky, Crunchy Breakfast Tempeh (p. 16), and perfect with Avocado Reubens (p. 25) for lunch. In other words, these are great anytime.

8 medium potatoes, boiled and mashed
1 cup unbleached all-purpose flour
Egg replacer equivalent of 1½ eggs
Salt to taste

Mix the potatoes, flour, egg replacer, and salt. Turn the mixture onto a floured bread board or countertop and knead into a dough, adding more flour if necessary until the dough is no longer sticky.

Roll the dough out to a ¾-inch thickness, then cut into 2-inch rounds (a drinking glass works well for this).

Lightly oil a frying pan or griddle and fry the rounds until browned on both sides, about 10 minutes. Serve with applesauce.

Serves 4   PREPARATION TIME: 30 minutes

SODA BREAD

No, we're not talking about cola. This baking soda bread is a winner. Try it!

2   cups whole wheat flour
2   cups unbleached all-purpose flour
1   teaspoon baking powder
1⅓ teaspoons baking soda
Dash of salt

2   tablespoons sugar
2   cups soy milk
3   tablespoons lemon juice or vinegar

Preheat the oven to 375 degrees.

Combine the whole wheat and all-purpose flours, baking powder, baking soda, salt, and sugar. Add the soy milk and lemon juice. Mix until dough forms—it should feel wet.

Turn the dough out onto a floured board and knead a few times, just until the dough sticks together. Form into a round loaf. Place on a greased cookie sheet and bake for 20 minutes.

Serve warm.

Makes 1 loaf   PREPARATION TIME: 20 minutes
                                  BAKING TIME: 20 minutes

MUFFINS

CORN MUFFINS

What's Everett's Blue Ribbon Chili (p. 134) without corn muffins?

1   cup cornmeal
1   cup sifted unbleached all-purpose flour
1   teaspoon salt
2½   teaspoons baking powder
1   cup soy milk
Egg replacer equivalent of 2 eggs, beaten
2   tablespoons (¼ stick) margarine, melted

Preheat the oven to 400 degrees. Lightly oil a muffin pan.

Sift the dry ingredients into a mixing bowl. In a small bowl, combine the soy milk and egg replacer, and add to the dry ingredients. Add the margarine and stir until blended. Pour the batter into the muffin pan, filling each muffin cup about two-thirds full. Bake for 20 minutes, or until an inserted toothpick or fork comes out clean.

Makes 10 to 12 muffins　　　PREPARATION TIME: 15 minutes
　　　　　　　　　　　　　　　BAKING TIME: 20 minutes

A-B-C MUFFINS

Apple juice, bananas, and cashews—so much flavor in a moist muffin. It's A-B-C-Divine!

2　　cups unbleached all-purpose flour
4　　teaspoons baking powder
½　　teaspoon ground cinnamon
½　　cup sugar
1½　cups apple juice
1　　medium apple, peeled, cored, and chopped
2　　ripe medium bananas, mashed
½　　cup cashews, chopped

Preheat the oven to 325 degrees. Lightly oil the muffin pan.

Combine the dry ingredients and mix well. Add the apple juice, apple, banana, and cashews and stir well. Pour the batter into the muffin pan, filling the muffin cups two-thirds full. Bake for 35 to 45 minutes, or until raised and lightly brown.

Makes 10 to 12 muffins　　　PREPARATION TIME: 20 minutes
　　　　　　　　　　　　　　　BAKING TIME: 35–45 minutes

BLUEBERRY–POPPY SEED MUFFINS

Moist and delicious, these muffins are bound to please. At breakfast, at noon, or any other time, treat yourself.

2	cups unbleached all-purpose flour
⅓	cup sugar
2	teaspoons baking powder
1½	teaspoons poppy seeds
¼	teaspoon salt
1	cup soy milk
4	tablespoons (½ stick) margarine, melted
Egg	replacer equivalent of 1 egg, beaten
¼	teaspoon grated lemon rind
1	teaspoon lemon juice
1	cup fresh or frozen blueberries, thawed and drained

Preheat the oven to 400 degrees. Lightly oil a muffin pan.

Combine the flour, sugar, baking powder, poppy seeds, and salt in a large bowl and stir until well blended. Add the soy milk, margarine, egg replacer, lemon rind, and lemon juice and stir until moistened. Fold in the blueberries.

Spoon the batter into the muffin pan, filling the cups two-thirds full. Bake for 20 to 25 minutes, or until the muffins are golden brown.

Makes 1 dozen　　　　　　　　PREPARATION TIME: 20 minutes
　　　　　　　　　　　　　　　BAKING TIME: 20–25 minutes

PUMPKIN MUFFINS

You don't have to wait until Halloween or Thanksgiving to make these scrumptious muffins; they're perfect all year 'round for a leisurely Sunday brunch or a midmorning pick-me-up at the office.

2¼ **cups unbleached all-purpose flour**
1   **cup packed dark brown sugar**
1   **tablespoon baking powder**
1   **teaspoon ground cinnamon**
¼   **teaspoon salt**
½   **teaspoon baking soda**
¼   **teaspoon grated nutmeg**
⅛   **teaspoon ground ginger or cloves**
1¼ **cups pumpkin puree (10 ounces)**
½   **cup soy milk**
Egg replacer equivalent of 2 eggs
⅓   **cup margarine**

Preheat the oven to 350 degrees. Lightly oil a muffin pan.

In a large bowl, mix 1 cup of the flour, the brown sugar, baking powder, cinnamon, salt, baking soda, nutmeg, and ginger or cloves. Add the pumpkin, soy milk, egg replacer, and margarine.

Beat with an electric mixer until blended. Add the remaining flour and beat well. Pour the batter into the muffin pan, filling the cups two-thirds full. Bake for 1 hour, or until an inserted toothpick or fork comes out clean.

Makes 1 dozen   PREPARATION TIME: 25 minutes
                                           BAKING TIME: 1 hour

RYE MUFFINS

You'll want to make these flavorful muffins often since you can't go awry with this easy recipe.

¾   **cup rye flour**
3   **tablespoons sugar**
¾   **cup unbleached all-purpose flour**
1   **tablespoon baking powder**
1   **teaspoon salt**
Egg replacer equivalent of 2 eggs
1   **tablespoon molasses**
1½ **cups soy milk**
1   **tablespoon caraway seeds**

Preheat the oven to 425 degrees. Lightly oil a muffin pan.

Place the dry ingredients in a bowl and mix well. Beat the egg replacer until it is foamy, then add the molasses and soy milk and stir well.

Make a well in the dry ingredients, pour in the soy milk mixture, and stir. Finally, stir in the caraway seeds. Spoon into the muffin pan, filling the cups about two-thirds full. Bake for 20 minutes, or until an inserted toothpick or fork comes out clean.

Makes 1 dozen   PREPARATION TIME: 20 minutes
                                   BAKING TIME: 20 minutes

9 MAIN COURSES

"The meat industry is huge, but kind people are making a difference. There are more vegetarians and vegans than ever. The example I try to set for family and friends as we share scrumptious vegan holiday meals has far-reaching effects for the animals."

—BELINDA CARLISLE

These exciting entrees show that a vegetarian diet is anything but bland. With spicy selections like jalepeño and bean burritos, vegetable curries, and vegetarian paella, you can "wow" skeptical friends and make your family sit up and take notice.

No one will ask "Where's the beef?" when you serve satisfying fare like a hearty Hungarian stew and herb-flavored lentils. And these low-fat meals won't slow you down the way heavy, meat-based dishes do. Even better, they won't slow down the planet, with the habitat destruction, soil erosion, and water pollution caused by meat production.

This chapter also includes recipes for old standbys like a meat(less) loaf, lasagna, macaroni and "cheese," and pasta primavera. So you needn't give up your favorites in the switch to a kinder, healthier diet. You won't give up any flavor or texture, either—just lots of cholesterol, fat, and guilt.

NORTH AMERICAN CUISINE

ROBIN'S POT PIE

Vegetables and tofu smothered in a creamy sauce surrounded by a flaky crust—what could be more ideal for those blustery days of winter?

1   8- or 9-inch pie crust, shell baked and dough
       for top crust kept chilled (Sister's Pie Crust, p. 188)
¼   cup unbleached all-purpose flour
1   tablespoon nutritional yeast flakes
1   teaspoon salt
¾   teaspoon garlic powder
3   cups firm tofu, cut into ¼-inch cubes
2   tablespoons vegetable oil
1   cup finely chopped onion
1   cup sliced celery
1   cup sliced carrots
1   cup of other vegetables (such as fresh or frozen corn, peas,
       green beans or whatever tempts your taste buds)
2   cups Chickenless Gravy (p. 111)

Set the pie shell aside. Combine the flour, yeast, salt, garlic powder, and tofu in a paper bag, and shake. Sauté the tofu mixture in the oil until lightly browned. Add the onion, celery, and carrots and continue to sauté until the onions are soft, about 5 minutes. Add the other vegetables and cook until the vegetables are tender but crisp, about 5 minutes.

Preheat the oven to 375 degrees. Pour the gravy over the mixture in the skillet and stir. Then pour into the pie shell. Roll out top dough and place on the pie. Bake for 30 minutes or until crust is lightly browned.

Serves 8   PREPARATION TIME: 45 minutes
                                  BAKING TIME: 30 minutes

Variation: For a different take on this dish, pour the vegetable mixture into an uncovered casserole dish and top with crushed cornflakes. Bake for 30 minutes.

VEGETARIAN BURGER LOAF WITH BROWN GRAVY

Pecans and cashews turn an ordinary loaf into a treasure of taste. The accompanying gravy also goes beautifully with grain and nut roasts and mashed potatoes.

For the loaf

2   tablespoons (¼ stick) margarine or water
½   cup diced onion
½   cup chopped celery
2   tablespoons chopped green bell pepper
1   clove garlic, crushed
1   20-ounce can vegetarian burger (see Glossary of Ingredients)
½   cup pecans, chopped fine
½   cup cashews, chopped fine
¼   cup bread crumbs
¼   teaspoon dried thyme
¼   teaspoon grated nutmeg

BROWN GRAVY

2   tablespoons (¼ stick) margarine
1   medium onion, diced
2   tablespoons unbleached all-purpose flour
1   teaspoon garlic salt
2   tablespoons cornstarch
1½ cups water or Vegetable Broth (p. 52)
1   teaspoon yeast extract (see Glossary of Ingredients)
1–2 tablespoons soy sauce or tamari
Pepper to taste

Preheat the oven to 375 degrees.

Heat the margarine or water in a medium frying pan over medium heat. Cook the onion, celery, green pepper, and garlic until the vegetables are tender, about 5 to 7 minutes.

In a large mixing bowl, combine the vegetables with the rest of the ingredients. Put into a greased baking dish and bake for 40 minutes.

Heat the margarine for the gravy in a medium saucepan over medium heat. Sauté the onion for a few minutes, then add the flour and garlic salt and sauté for another 8 to 9 minutes. Dissolve the cornstarch in the water or broth. Gradually add the cornstarch mixture to the onion mixture, bring to a boil, then simmer for 10 minutes. Strain the gravy into a separate saucepan and add the yeast extract, soy sauce, and pepper. Simmer for another minute or two, stirring constantly. Keep warm.

Serve loaf with gravy.

Serves 6   PREPARATION TIME: 45 minutes
                                  BAKING TIME: 40 minutes

LENTIL-RICE ROAST WITH CASHEW GRAVY

A moist, savory main course smothered in a cashew gravy that's perfect for a holiday feast.

1½ **cups lentils**
1½ **cups millet**
1½ **cups brown rice**
9   **cups water**
1   **cup bread crumbs**
½   **cup rolled oats**
½   **cup cashews, finely ground**
¼   **cup vegetable oil**
3   **tablespoons onion powder**
1½ **tablespoons crumbled sage**
½   **teaspoon celery seed**
Salt to taste
Garlic powder (optional)

CASHEW GRAVY

2   **cups water**
½   **cup cashews**
2   **tablespoons cornstarch**
2   **tablespoons onion powder**
½   **teaspoon salt**

Pick over the lentils, then combine in a saucepan with the millet, rice, and water. Bring to a boil, lower the heat, and simmer until cooked, about 1 hour.

Preheat the oven to 350 degrees. Lightly oil two 8½ × 4½-inch loaf pans.

Add the remaining loaf ingredients and mix well. Transfer mixture to loaf pans and bake for 1 hour, or until lightly brown and the top is dry to the touch.

Make gravy. Place ingredients in a blender and liquify. In a medium sauté pan over medium heat, heat the gravy, stirring constantly, until thick. Add more water if the gravy becomes too thick. Keep warm.

Serves 12 to 16   PREPARATION TIME: 1½ hours
                                  BAKING TIME: 1 hour

MOCK CHICKEN LOAF FLORENTINE WITH CHICKENLESS GRAVY

The "fooled you" taste and texture of chicken in a savory loaf, smothered in a cheesy-tasting chickenless gravy. Yum!

For the loaf

1   10-ounce package frozen spinach, thawed
2   tablespoons vegetable oil or water
1   small onion, finely chopped
2   tablespoons imitation chicken-flavored powder,
        or 1 vegetable bouillon cube
1¾ cups boiling water
2   cups TVP granules (see Glossary of Ingredients)
1   pound soft tofu
1   cup gluten flour or ¾ cup whole wheat flour
1   tablespoon nutritional yeast flakes
1½ teaspoons salt
1   teaspoon garlic powder
1   teaspoon poultry seasoning
½   teaspoon onion powder
3   tablespoons vegetable oil

CHICKENLESS GRAVY

2   cups boiling water
2   tablespoons vegetable oil
3   tablespoons nutritional yeast
1   vegetable bouillon cube
½ cup diced fresh mushrooms
½ cup finely chopped onion
Onion salt to taste
Unbleached all-purpose flour

Steam the spinach and drain well.

Heat the oil or water in a medium frying pan over medium heat. Cook the onion, stirring occasionally, until transparent, about 5 minutes.

Dissolve the imitation chicken-flavored powder or bouillon powder in the boiling water. Add the TVP and let stand for about 10 minutes.

Preheat the oven to 350 degrees.

Pat the tofu dry, then mash. In a large bowl, combine the TVP mixture, spinach, and tofu. Stir in the remaining ingredients and pour the mixture into a lightly greased 8½ × 4½-inch loaf pan. Smooth the top and bake for 45 minutes, or until brown on top.

If the loaf begins to get too brown on top, cover with aluminum foil. Make the gravy. In a large saucepan, simmer all the ingredients except the flour for approximately 5 minutes. Slowly add the flour (tablespoon by tablespoon), whisking after each addition, until desired thickness is reached. Keep warm.

Let loaf stand for 10 minutes, then run a knife around the edges and turn out onto a platter. Serve with gravy.

Serves 6 to 8   PREPARATION TIME: 45 minutes
                                         BAKING TIME: 45 minutes

BETH'S LENTILS

With thyme and parsley to give the lentils a fresh-from-the-garden flavor, this dish, with bread and salad accompaniments, makes a satisfying supper. Bring leftovers to work for a hearty, hunger-busting lunch.

2 tablespoons olive oil or water
2 large onions, diced
1 medium carrot, sliced
½ teaspoon dried thyme
½ teaspoon dried marjoram
3 cups Vegetable Broth (p. 52) or water
1 cup lentils, rinsed
Salt to taste
¼ cup chopped fresh parsley
2 14-ounce cans stewed tomatoes

Heat the oil or water in a medium frying pan over medium heat. Cook the onion and carrot for 3 to 5 minutes, then add the herbs and sauté 1 minute longer.

Add all the other ingredients, bring to a boil, cover, and reduce the heat to a simmer. Cook until the lentils are tender, about 50 minutes.

Serves 4 to 6   PREPARATION TIME: 10 minutes
                                   COOKING TIME: 50 minutes

BBQ CHICKPEAS

A simple way to jazz up chickpeas—perfect for a hearty dinner or a potluck picnic lunch.

2   **16-ounce cans chickpeas, rinsed and drained**
1   **16-ounce jar (2 cups) commercial spaghetti sauce**
⅓   **cup molasses**
¼   **cup finely chopped onions**

Preheat the oven to 350 degrees. Oil a casserole dish.

In a large bowl, combine all the ingredients and mix well. Pour into the 2-quart casserole dish, cover, and bake for approximately 1 hour, or until sauce has darkened and thickened.

Serve over noodles or rice.

Serves 6   PREPARATION TIME: 10 minutes
                                    BAKING TIME: 1 hour

KATIE'S TOFU PASTA SAUCE

This easy sauce is also good over rice or potatoes for a simple supper after a long day.

2 **tablespoons olive oil**
1 **pound firm tofu, cut into ¼-inch cubes**
1 **medium onion, diced**
1 **tablespoon soy sauce or tamari**
1 **cup frozen peas, thawed**
Fresh or dried parsley

Heat the olive oil in a medium frying pan over medium heat. Sauté the tofu and onion until the onion becomes soft, about 5 minutes.

Add the soy sauce and peas and continue to cook over low heat until heated through. Serve over your favorite pasta and garnish with fresh or dried parsley.

Serves 4 to 6   PREPARATION TIME: 25 minutes

CELENE'S CELESTIAL STEW

A taste of Celene's stew will have you floating among the stars.

2   pounds potatoes, chopped into cubes
2   28-ounce cans whole peeled tomatoes
2   medium onions, diced
3   medium carrots, sliced
1   pound bag frozen corn kernels
1   pound bag frozen peas
1   cup dry sherry
2   tablespoons plus 1 teaspoon garlic powder
2   teaspoons dried oregano
1   tablespoon minced fresh basil
1   teaspoon dried rosemary
2   bay leaves
1   teaspoon dried thyme
½   teaspoon crumbled sage
2   teaspoons minced fresh parsley
2   teaspoons salt

Boil the potatoes until soft, about 20 to 25 minutes. Pour off the water and add the 2 cans of tomatoes and the juice from the tomatoes. Add the onions, carrots, corn, and peas. Stir well and cook for about 5 minutes.

Add the remaining ingredients and cook uncovered at a low heat for about 2 hours.

Serves 8 to 10   PREPARATION TIME: 25 minutes
                         COOKING TIME: 2½ hours

STUFFED ACORN SQUASH

Mildly sweet and savory, this eye-catching entree looks splendid on your holiday buffet table.

3	acorn squash, sliced in half, seeds removed
2	tablespoons (¼ stick) margarine, melted
2	tablespoons olive oil or water
1	small onion, finely chopped
2	stalks celery, finely chopped
2	medium apples, peeled and finely chopped
¼	cup pure maple syrup
½	cup raisins (optional)

¼–½ teaspoon each dried parsley, sage, rosemary, and thyme
Salt and pepper to taste
1   package vegan cornbread stuffing
Chickenless Gravy (p. 111)

Preheat the oven to 400 degrees.

Brush the inside of the squash with the melted margarine and set aside.

Heat the olive oil or water in a medium frying pan over medium heat. Cook the onion, celery, and apple for about 8 minutes. Then add the maple syrup, raisins if using, herbs, salt, and pepper. Mix well.

In a large bowl, mix the cornbread stuffing and the vegetable mixture. Spoon into each squash half, cover with foil, and bake about 40 to 45 minutes, or until squash is tender. Serve with Chickenless Gravy.

Serves 4 to 6
PREPARATION TIME: 20 minutes
BAKING TIME: 40–45 minutes

STUFFED EGGPLANT

You'll be stuffed when you finish this dish, but you won't regret a single bite.

2	medium eggplants
1¼	teaspoons salt
2	tablespoons chopped cashews
2	tablespoons olive oil
1	cup finely chopped onions
3	cloves garlic, minced
4	plum tomatoes, chopped
⅓	cup raisins
1	tablespoon drained capers
½	teaspoon pepper
3	tablespoons chopped fresh parsley
½	teaspoon red wine vinegar

Cut the eggplants in half lengthwise, and make 6 lengthwise slits into the "flesh" of each half, cutting deeply but not through the skin. Sprinkle 1 teaspoon of the salt on the eggplant halves, allowing salt to fall into the slits. Then place the eggplant halves cut side down in a colander. Set aside for at least 30 minutes to release any bitterness.

In a medium frying pan over medium heat, toast the cashew pieces until golden brown, then remove from the pan and set aside.

Heat 1 tablespoon of the olive oil in the same frying pan over medium heat. Sauté the onions and garlic until the onions are golden, about 5 minutes. Stir in the tomatoes, raisins, capers, pepper, and remaining salt. Cover and cook, stirring often, until tomatoes soften, 10 to 12 minutes.

Preheat the oven to 350 degrees. Lightly oil a baking sheet.

Add 2 tablespoons parsley, the rest of the oil, the cashew nuts, and the vinegar to the mixture in the frying pan and stir until well blended.

Squeeze any moisture from the eggplants. Spread the mixture over the top of the eggplants and bake for 45 minutes. Sprinkle with the rest of the parsley and serve.

Serves 4   PREPARATION TIME: 1 hour
                                            BAKING TIME: 45 minutes

SPINACH RING WITH CREAMED ONIONS

This spinach mold is as savory as it looks.

2   **pounds fresh spinach**
1   **teaspoon dried rosemary**
1   **tablespoon chopped fresh parsley**
1   **tablespoon minced onion**
2   **tablespoons (¼ stick) margarine**
Salt and pepper to taste
15–20   **pearl onions**
2   **tablespoons unbleached all-purpose flour**
½   **teaspoon salt**
1¼   **cups soy milk**

Wash the spinach and chop the leaves. In a heavy pot, combine the spinach, rosemary, parsley, onion, and margarine. Cover and simmer over medium heat until tender, about 5 to 7 minutes. Season the spinach with the salt and pepper. Squeeze out all the juice and pack the spinach firmly into a greased 1-quart ring mold. Set aside.

Preheat the oven to 350 degrees.

Cook the pearl onions in boiling salted water until tender, about 15 to 20 minutes. Meanwhile, pour the flour, salt, and soy milk into a blender and process until smooth. Pour the mixture into a saucepan and heat until thick (adding flour if necessary). Drain the onions and add to the cream sauce and heat through.

Place the spinach mold into a pan of hot water, cover, and place in the oven until heated through, about 15 minutes. Unmold onto a large platter and fill the center with the creamed onions. Serve immediately.

Serves 6   PREPARATION TIME: 1¼ hours
                                        BAKING TIME: 15 minutes

BROCCOLI AND RICE CASSEROLE

The nutritional yeast gives this casserole a "cheesy" quality, the broccoli gives it color, and the spices give it pizzazz.

1	10-ounce package frozen broccoli florets, or 1 bunch fresh, cut into florets
2	cups white rice
½	cup (1 stick) margarine
½	cup unbleached all-purpose flour
3½	cups boiling water
2	teaspoons salt
1	tablespoon soy sauce or tamari
1½	teaspoons garlic powder

1   **teaspoon onion powder**
Pinch of turmeric
1   **cup of nutritional yeast flakes**
Salt and pepper to taste
Pinch of paprika

Steam the broccoli, about 6 minutes. Prepare the rice according to the package directions.

Spread the cooked rice evenly over the bottom of a 9 × 13-inch baking dish. Sprinkle the broccoli over the rice and set aside.

Preheat the oven to 350 degrees.

Melt the margarine in a medium frying pan over low heat. Beat in the flour with a whisk over medium heat until the mixture is smooth and bubbly, then whisk in the boiling water, salt, soy sauce, garlic and onion powders, and turmeric. Cook the sauce until it thickens and bubbles, then whip in the yeast. Add salt and pepper to taste.

Pour the sauce over the broccoli and rice, sprinkle the top with paprika, and bake for 15 minutes. If desired, place pan under broiler for a few minutes until the sauce is browned and crusty.

Serves 4   PREPARATION TIME: 30 minutes
                                        BAKING TIME: 15 minutes

CHEEZY MACARONI CASSEROLE

Nutritional yeast turns a high-fat American staple into a more health-ful but equally delicious main dish. A fresh, crunchy salad rounds out the meal.

½   cup nutritional yeast flakes
⅓   cup unbleached all-purpose flour
1   cup Vegetable Broth (p. 52)
Up to 1½ cups water
1½ tablespoons soy sauce or tamari
½   teaspoon garlic powder
¼   teaspoon paprika
¼   teaspoon dried basil
¼   teaspoon dried oregano
1   4-ounce can tomato sauce
2   cups elbow macaroni, cooked according to package directions

Preheat the oven to 350 degrees.

Combine the yeast and the flour in a medium saucepan. Place the mixture over low heat, stirring until lightly toasted. Slowly add the broth, stirring to make a thick batter. Add water ¼ cup at a time until the sauce is smooth and slightly thick. Add the remaining ingredients except the macaroni, and stir well.

Place the cooked macaroni in a casserole dish and stir in the sauce. Bake for 30 minutes, or until sauce bubbles.

Serves 4 to 6   PREPARATION TIME: 15 minutes
                                   BAKING TIME: 30 minutes

ASIAN CUISINE

CHINESE STIR-FRY

If you keep cooked rice on hand, you'll find that few meals are simpler to prepare or faster to cook than a vegetable stir-fry.

1   tablespoon vegetable oil
1   thin slice fresh ginger, slightly mashed
1   clove garlic, minced
¼   cup water
4   tablespoons tamari or soy sauce
1   cup chopped broccoli, in bite-sized pieces
½   cup thinly sliced water chestnuts
½   cup bamboo shoots
½   cup mung bean sprouts
½   cup halved fresh mushrooms
1   cup snow peas

Heat the oil in a medium frying pan over medium heat. Sauté the ginger and garlic for 3 minutes, then remove the ginger.

Add the water, soy sauce, and broccoli. Stir over medium heat for 5 to 7 minutes, then add the remaining vegetables. Stir-fry for another 5 minutes, or until all the ingredients are combined and heated through. Add additional soy sauce to taste. Serve over rice.

Serves 4   PREPARATION TIME: 40 minutes

SWEET AND SOUR TOFU WITH VEGETABLES

The gourmet taste will fool them—they'll think you fussed over a hot wok for hours.

1   tablespoon cornstarch
¾   cup Vegetable Broth (p. 52) or water
3   tablespoons white wine vinegar
3   tablespoons sugar
1   tablespoon ketchup
2   tablespoons soy sauce or tamari
½   teaspoon ground ginger
¼   teaspoon cayenne pepper (optional)
2   tablespoons vegetable oil
2   cloves garlic, crushed
1   medium onion, thinly sliced
2   medium carrots, cut into matchstick shapes
1   green bell pepper, sliced into strips
1   stalk celery, chopped into strips
½   cup sliced fresh mushrooms
1   pound tofu, cut into strips

Mix the cornstarch with 3 tablespoons of the broth or water in a small cup until well blended. Add the rest of the stock, vinegar, sugar, ketchup, soy sauce, ginger, and cayenne pepper, and set aside.

Heat the oil in a wok or large frying pan over high heat. Stir-fry the garlic, onion, and carrots until the carrots begin to soften, about 5 minutes. Add the pepper, celery, and mushrooms, and stir-fry for another 2 to 3 minutes.

Stir the sauce well and add to the vegetables. Cook until the mixture thickens. Add the tofu and cook until the tofu is thoroughly heated. Serve immediately over rice.

Serves 4 to 6   PREPARATION TIME: 30 minutes

VEGETARIAN SUSHI

Now you can make this delicacy at home and impress your family and friends with your mastery of Japanese cuisine!

6   cups water
3   cups short-grain brown rice
1   small cucumber, seeded and julienned
1   small zucchini, julienned
1   small yellow summer squash, julienned
½   green bell pepper, julienned
½   red bell pepper, julienned
½   pound fresh spinach
2   small carrots, julienned
2–3 tablespoons rice wine vinegar
1   tablespoon brown sugar
1   package nori (dried seaweed) (see Glossary of Ingredients)
Wasabi paste, or wasabi powder prepared according to package
   directions (see Glossary of Ingredients)

Bring the water to a boil. Add the rice, lower the heat, and simmer, stirring occasionally, so that the rice becomes sticky. Simmer for 40 minutes or until the rice is tender.

While the rice is cooking, steam the vegetables over boiling water about 5 to 7 minutes. Let cool to room temperature.

When the rice is cooked, stir in the vinegar and brown sugar, and cool to room temperature.

When the vegetables and rice are cool enough to handle, lay out the first nori sheet. Place a handful of rice in the center of the sheet, moisten your hands with water, and gently but firmly press the rice to the edges of the sheet so that there is a thin layer of rice on the sheet.

Begin constructing each sushi roll by spreading a bit of wasabi paste on top of the rice approximately 1½ inches from one edge of the nori. Lay the vegetable strips horizontally in a width of approximately 1 inch along the wasabi line. Carefully wrap the closest edge over the vegetables, then roll the nori delicately but tightly. If you have a bamboo sushi mat roll it around the sushi roll and compress gently. Once it is completely rolled, slice the roll into 6 pieces and arrange on a platter. Repeat with remaining nori sheets.

Makes 6 rolls   PREPARATION TIME: 1½ hours

ORIENTAL SPAGHETTI

Liven up your spaghetti with crunchy cucumbers and hot chili oil for the perfect summertime supper!

Reprinted with permission from the Physicians Committee for Responsible Medicine.

1   **pound thin spaghetti**
2   **tablespoons roasted sesame oil**
4   **tablespoons soy sauce or tamari**
1   **cup snow peas**
2   **cucumbers, peeled, seeded, and cut into strips**
       ¼ inch x 1½ inches
¾   **cup thinly sliced green onions**
3   **tablespoons chopped fresh parsley**
2   **tablespoons red wine vinegar**
1   **teaspoon dry mustard**
1   **teaspoon hot chili oil**

Cook the spaghetti according to the package directions and drain. Combine 1 tablespoon of the sesame oil with 2 tablespoons of the soy sauce. Toss the warm spaghetti with this mixture and set aside.
    Steam the snow peas for 2 minutes. Drain and cool under cold

water. Combine the snow peas, cucumber strips, green onions, and parsley.

Stir together the remaining sesame oil, soy sauce, vinegar, mustard, and chili oil. Toss this sauce with the vegetables. Then toss the vegetable mixture with the spaghetti mixture. Serve cold.

Serves 4 to 6   PREPARATION TIME: 30 minutes

NOODLES AND VEGETABLES WITH PEANUT SAUCE

This elegant oriental main dish makes easy-to-serve party fare.

1   **pound spaghetti noodles**
½   **cup peanuts**
2   **cloves garlic**
2   **tablespoons soy sauce or tamari**
4   **teaspoons distilled white vinegar**
1   **tablespoon sugar**
⅛   **teaspoon cayenne pepper**
½   **cup water**
2   **medium carrots, julienned**
½   **pound (1 cup) snowpeas, sliced**
¼   **cup roasted sesame oil**
2   **green onions, chopped**
1   **cucumber, peeled, seeded, and julienned**

Cook the spaghetti according to the package directions.

In a blender or food processor, combine the peanuts, garlic, soy sauce, vinegar, sugar, cayenne pepper, and water. Blend until smooth and set aside.

Steam the carrots and the snow peas until tender-crisp, about 7 minutes, and set aside.

Rinse the spaghetti with cold water and drain thoroughly. Pour into a large mixing bowl. Toss with the sesame oil.

Add the peanut sauce, carrots, and snowpeas and toss. Just before serving, top with the green onions and cucumber.

Serves 3 to 4   PREPARATION TIME: 30 minutes

k.d. lang's INDONESIAN SALAD WITH SPICY PEANUT DRESSING

The best of the East comes west in this exciting main dish salad.

For the salad

3   tablespoons vegetable oil
Salt to taste
1   pound firm tofu, patted dry and cut into ¼-inch cubes
2   small potatoes, boiled and cut into bite-size wedges
½   pound fresh spinach, cleaned, steamed, and chopped
½   small head green cabbage, shredded and lightly steamed
½   pound mung bean sprouts, washed thoroughly

For the dressing

4   cloves garlic
¼   cup roasted peanuts
5   teaspoons soy sauce or tamari
3   tablespoons lime or lemon juice
4   teaspoons brown sugar
¼   teaspoon cayenne pepper
2   tablespoons water

Heat the oil and salt in a medium frying pan over medium heat. Add the tofu in small batches and sauté until lightly browned on both sides, about 5 minutes. Remove with a slotted spoon and drain on a paper towel.

Arrange the bean curd, potatoes, spinach, and cabbage on individual plates.

Prepare the dressing by placing all of the dressing ingredients in a blender and blending until smooth. If the dressing seems too thick, add another teaspoon of water.

Top the vegetables and bean curd with the bean sprouts and dressing, and serve immediately.

Serves 6   PREPARATION TIME: 1 hour

VEGGIES TAJ MAHAL

The savory spices of Indian cuisine make this dish scrumptious. Serve on a bed of rice or scoop up with triangles of pita bread. Visit your friendly neighborhood health food or gourmet store and pick up some tangy chutneys to complement the meal.

1   tablespoon vegetable oil
1   tablespoon margarine
2   cloves garlic, minced
¾   teaspoon ground cinnamon
½   teaspoon ground cardamom
1½   teaspoons ground cumin
1   tablespoon minced fresh coriander
½   teaspoon fennel seeds
¾   teaspoon turmeric
2   teaspoons ground ginger
½   teaspoon cayenne pepper
1½   cups chopped onions
1   cup chopped tomatoes
⅔   cup sliced carrots
1   cup frozen peas, thawed
2   cups potatoes (white and/or sweet), peeled and diced
Salt to taste
¾   cup water
¼   cup slivered almonds

Heat the oil and the margarine in a large frying pan over medium heat. Add the garlic and the spices all at once, and reduce the heat to low. Cook for approximately 1 minute, making sure not to burn the spices.

Add the onions and sauté for a few more minutes, until soft. Add the tomatoes and stir in the carrots, peas, potatoes, salt, and water. Bring the vegetables to a boil, cover, and reduce the heat to a simmer. Cook until the potatoes are soft, about 15 to 20 minutes.

Serve the veggies over a bed of rice and garnish with slivered almonds.

Serves 6   PREPARATION TIME: 30 minutes
                                     COOKING TIME: 15–20 minutes

KASHMIRI STIR-FRY

Turn the everyday stir-fry into something exotic with this exciting but easy recipe from the land of lakes and mountains.

2   tablespoons vegetable oil
1   large eggplant, cut into long, thin slices
1   head broccoli, cut into bite-size pieces
1   teaspoon salt
1   pinch asafetida (see Glossary of Ingredients)
¼   teaspoon cayenne pepper
¼   teaspoon paprika
2–4 tablespoons water

Heat the oil in a wok or frying pan over high heat. Add the eggplant and fry until lightly browned. Remove the eggplant and place on a paper towel to soak up excess oil.

Fry the broccoli in the same pan for 3 minutes. Add the salt and asafetida, and continue frying. Add the cayenne pepper, paprika, and cooked eggplant and stir until well mixed.

Add 2 to 4 tablespoons of water, lower the heat, and cook, covered, until broccoli is tender and everything is heated through, about 5 to 7 minutes.

Serve over rice.

Serves 4   PREPARATION TIME: 20 minutes

CAULIFLOWER CURRY

For a taste of India, try this spicy cauliflower delight.

1½   teaspoons grated fresh ginger
½   cup grated coconut
3   tablespoons roasted peanuts
2   tablespoons sesame seeds
3–4 cloves garlic
1   tablespoon ground cumin
1   teaspoon ground cloves
1   teaspoon turmeric
½   teaspoon cayenne pepper
1   tablespoon vegetable oil
2   medium onions, chopped
1   medium cauliflower, cut into small pieces
1½   tablespoons lemon juice

Put the ginger, coconut, peanuts, sesame seeds, garlic, and spices in a blender with a small amount of water and blend until smooth; set aside.

Heat the oil in a medium frying pan over medium heat. Sauté the onions until translucent, about 5 to 7 minutes. Add the cauliflower and a pinch of salt and stir until well mixed.

Add the spice mixture to the cauliflower and onions, and cook on low heat, covered, stirring every few minutes, until the cauliflower is tender (add a little water, if needed), about 12 to 15 minutes.

Add the lemon juice and cook for 3 more minutes. Serve over rice.

Serves 4 to 6   PREPARATION TIME: 30 minutes

INDIAN-STYLE CHICKPEA CASSEROLE

Full of exotic flavor, this simple curry dish is an excellent introduction to Indian cuisine.

1	tablespoon vegetable oil or water
½-1	cup chopped onions
2	cloves garlic, finely chopped
1	bay leaf
1	cup cooked brown or white rice
1	cup canned cream-style corn
1	16-ounce can chickpeas, rinsed and drained
2	teaspoons curry powder
½	teaspoon turmeric
½	teaspoon ground cumin
¼	cup water

Preheat the oven to 375 degrees. Lightly oil a 1½-quart baking dish.

Heat the oil or water in a large frying pan over medium heat. Cook the onions, garlic, and bay leaf, stirring frequently, until the onions are tender, about 5 minutes. Remove the pan from the heat and discard the bay leaf. Add the remaining ingredients and mix well.

Spoon the chickpea mixture into the prepared baking dish. Bake, covered, for 30 minutes, or until sauce bubbles.

Serves 6   PREPARATION TIME: 15 minutes
       BAKING TIME: 30 minutes

CHANA MASALA

A careful blend of spices is what makes this chickpea dish special.

2   16-ounce cans chickpeas, drained
2   cups water
½   teaspoon salt
2½   teaspoons chana masala (see Glossary of Ingredients); or
        ½ teaspoon ground cumin, 1 teaspoon ground coriander, ½
        teaspoon garam masala, and ¼ teaspoon amchur
¼   teaspoon turmeric

Boil the chickpeas and water in a large saucepan, then turn the heat to low and add the salt and the spices. Continue to simmer the chickpeas on low heat for 5 to 10 minutes, or until the curry thickens.
    Serve over rice.

Serves 4 to 6   PREPARATION TIME: 25 minutes

OH, DAHL-ING!

Dahl, a traditional Indian side dish, also makes a terrific main course.

2   cups water
1   cup green lentils, rinsed and sorted
3   medium potatoes, peeled and chopped into bite-size wedges
3   tablespoons margarine
1   medium onion, finely chopped
1½   tablespoons curry powder (or to taste)
1   teaspoon ground coriander
½   teaspoon turmeric
½   teaspoon dried parsley
Salt and pepper to taste

Bring water to a rapid boil. Simmer lentils in the water, covered, over low heat for 45 minutes, or until the water is absorbed.

In a separate pot, boil the potatoes until soft, about 15 to 20 minutes.

Heat the margarine in a medium frying pan over medium heat. Sauté the onion, curry powder, coriander, turmeric, parsley, salt, and pepper for 10 minutes over low heat (do not brown the onion).

Combine the cooked lentils, boiled potatoes, and onion mixture. Serve immediately over rice.

Serves 6   PREPARATION TIME: 1 hour

SOUTH AMERICAN, CARIBBEAN, AND MEXICAN CUISINE

BEAN BURRITOS WITH SALSA MEXICANA

An all-around winner, perfect as part of a theme dinner or buffet but sensational enough to go solo. Salsa adds the perfect finishing touch, whether it's fresh, chunky, and homemade or your favorite commercial brand perked up with a little fresh coriander (cilantro). With Spanish rice, guacamole, and tofu sour cream, it's a fiesta of flavor.

10 flour tortillas
2½ cups dried pinto beans
6   cups water
2   medium onions, diced
Pinch of salt (optional)

Salsa Mexicana

1½ ripe medium tomatoes, diced
¼   cup diced jalapeño peppers

½   medium onion, diced
1   tablespoon chopped fresh coriander (cilantro)
1   green onion, chopped

Wash and drain the beans. In a large pot bring the beans, water, onions, and salt to a boil. Lower the heat, cover, and simmer, adding more water if necessary, until the beans are tender and will mash easily (approximately 3 hours).

Blend the ingredients for the salsa in a small bowl. Set aside.

Drain and mash the beans with a potato masher or an electric mixer.

Preheat oven to 350 degrees. Wrap the tortillas in foil and heat in oven for 8 to 10 minutes. Spoon some of the bean mixture onto each tortilla, top with green onions and salsa, and roll into a burrito.

Makes 10 burritos and 1½ cups salsa   PREPARATION TIME: ½ hour
                                          COOKING TIME: 3 hours

KEVIN AND LINDA NEALON'S DELICIOUS AND SIMPLE CHILI

When PETA asked its members to send in their favorite recipes, who should respond but Kevin Nealon from "Saturday Night Live" and his wife Linda! This is their favorite veggie chili recipe.

1   tablespoon olive oil
1   large onion, diced
½   green bell pepper, chopped
3   28-ounce cans crushed tomatoes
2   40-ounce cans dark red kidney beans, drained
3   tablespoons chili powder (or to taste)
1   teaspoon salt
1   tablespoon sugar (optional)

Heat the olive oil in a very large frying pan or Dutch oven over medium heat. Sauté the onions and pepper until tender, about 5 to 7 minutes.

Add the remaining ingredients and bring the mixture to a boil. Lower the heat and simmer, covered, for 1 hour.

Serves 8   PREPARATION TIME: 10 minutes

                                        COOKING TIME: 1 hour

EVERETT'S BLUE RIBBON CHILI

No chuckwagon supper ever had more come-'n'-get-it appeal than this hearty chili.

3   tablespoons vegetable oil
1   pound firm tofu, mashed
2   large sweet onions, diced
1   green bell pepper, diced
Garlic to taste
2   4-ounce cans mushrooms
6   tablespoons chili powder (or to taste)
Salt and pepper to taste
¼   teaspoon cayenne pepper
¼   teaspoon ground cumin
1   14-ounce can tomato sauce
2   28-ounce cans whole peeled tomatoes, with liquid
1   52-ounce can red kidney beans, drained and rinsed
3   tablespoons sugar

Heat the oil in a Dutch oven over medium heat. Sauté the tofu for 3 minutes; add the onions, green pepper, garlic, mushrooms, chili powder, salt, pepper, cayenne, and cumin. Cook until the vegetables are tender, about 5 to 7 minutes.

Add the tomato sauce, whole tomatoes, beans, and sugar. Simmer for about 1 hour. Serve with or without rice.

Serves 8   PREPARATION TIME: 15 minutes
                                    COOKING TIME: 1 hour

FRIJOLES NEGROS

Beans and rice never looked so good; this recipe shows how a simple dish can be turned into something special—perfect for dinner on cold winter nights.

1   **pound dried black beans**
2   **green bell peppers, halved and seeded**
8   **cups water**
1   **medium onion, quartered**
2   **cloves garlic**
1   **teaspoon dried oregano**
1   **teaspoon ground cumin**
1   **bay leaf**
Salt to taste
¼   **cup dry white wine**
1   **tablespoon red wine vinegar**
1   **tablespoon sugar**
¼   **cup olive oil (optional)**

Soak the beans with one of the green peppers in the water for 8 hours or overnight. After soaking, bring the beans, pepper, and water to a boil, then immediately turn the heat to simmer and cook, covered, for 1½ hours, or until the beans are almost tender.

Prepare a sauce, called *sofrito*, by combining the other green bell pepper, the onion, garlic, oregano, cumin, bay leaf, and a little of the cooking water in a blender. Blend on low until the mixture is smooth. Add the *sofrito* to the beans. Bring to a boil again, then immediately reduce the heat to a simmer.

Add salt and the wine, vinegar, and sugar. Continue to simmer, uncovered, until the bean mixture becomes thick, about 2 more hours, stirring occasionally.

If desired, add the olive oil immediately before serving. Serve over steamed rice.

Serves 6　　　　　　　　　　PREPARATION TIME: ½ hour
　　　　　　　　　　　　　　COOKING TIME: 3½ hours
　　　　　　　　　　　　　　SOAKING TIME: 8 hours

HAITIAN RED BEANS AND RICE

Make a meal with exotic appeal. It may look like a simple dish, but it sure doesn't taste like one.

1 pound dried kidney beans
3 tablespoons vegetable oil
2 cloves garlic, chopped or pressed
2 cups white rice
Several whole cloves

Soak the beans in a large pot or bowl of water to cover for 8 hours or overnight. Drain the beans, cover with fresh water, and bring to a boil. Turn the heat to low and simmer for 1½ to 2 hours, or until the beans are fairly soft.

Drain the beans and set the reserved cooking water aside. Add the oil to the pot and fry the beans with the garlic for a few minutes. Try not to stir too much or the beans will get mushy. (Add more oil if necessary.)

Return the water to the pot of beans and garlic and bring to a boil. If necessary, add more water to make 4 cups. Add the rice and cloves, and stir. Cover and simmer until the rice is cooked, about 25 to 30 minutes.

Serves 6   PREPARATION TIME: ½ hour
                                        COOKING TIME: 2–2½ hours
                                        SOAKING TIME: 8 hours

SPICY BLACK BEANS

Another bean dish! This one is hot, hot, hot! Serve it with Creole-style Chunky Rice (p. 180) and savor the flavor of south-of-the-border cuisine.

¾   **pound dried black beans**
4   **cups water**
2   **tablespoons vegetable oil**
1¼ **cups chopped onions**
2   **cloves garlic, minced**
2   **bay leaves**
1   **vegetable bouillon cube**
½   **teaspoon dried oregano**
½   **teaspoon hot sauce (or to taste)**
1   **tablespoon sugar**

Sort and wash the beans. Pour the beans and 2 cups of water into a medium saucepan and bring to a boil. Cover, remove from the heat, and let stand for 1 hour. Drain the beans and set aside.

Heat the oil in a large saucepan over medium-high heat until hot. Sauté the onions and garlic until the onions are tender, about 5 minutes.

Add the beans, remaining water, bay leaves, bouillon cube, oregano, hot sauce, and sugar. Bring to a boil, cover, reduce the heat, and simmer for 2 hours, or until the beans are tender.

Remove and discard the bay leaves. Serve over white or brown rice.

Serves 6 to 8   PREPARATION TIME: ½ hour

COOKING AND SOAKING TIME: 3 hours

VEGETARIAN PAELLA

Try this colorful, satisfying rice dish adapted from traditional Spanish fare.

1 **cup white rice**
2 **cups boiling water**
1 **tablespoon olive oil**
1 **small onion, chopped**
3 **cloves garlic, minced**
1 **green bell pepper, sliced**
1 **red bell pepper, sliced**
1 **ripe medium tomato, diced**
2 **cups water or Vegetable Broth (p. 52)**
1 **teaspoon salt**
1 **tablespoon paprika**
1 **teaspoon turmeric**
1 **cup frozen peas**
1 **cup artichoke hearts, drained and quartered**
¼ **cup sliced pimiento**

Mix the rice and boiling water and let stand for 20 minutes, then pour off the water.

In the meantime, heat the oil in a large frying pan over medium heat and sauté the onion and garlic until the onion is transparent, about 5 minutes. Add the peppers and tomato, and continue to sauté over medium heat for 3 minutes. Add the rice and water or broth. Bring to a boil, then reduce the heat to simmer. Add the salt, paprika, and turmeric. Cover and simmer until the rice is tender, about 20 minutes.

Add the peas and artichoke hearts, and cook about 1 minute longer. Turn out onto serving dish and garnish with pimiento.

Serves 4   PREPARATION TIME: 45 minutes

MEXICAN PIE

Here's chili and cornbread—always a popular combination—all in the same delicious dish.

2   **tablespoons water or vegetable oil**
1   **medium onion, diced**
1   **green bell pepper, chopped**
2   **cups frozen corn kernels**
1   **small can green chilies, chopped**
1   **cup tomato sauce**
2   **tablespoons chili powder**
Salt and pepper to taste
4   **cups cooked kidney beans, mashed**
1½   **cups cornmeal**
½   **cup unbleached all-purpose flour**
½   **teaspoon baking powder**
3   **cups water**

Heat the water or oil in a large pot over medium heat and cook the onion for 10 minutes. Add the green pepper, corn, green chilies, tomato sauce, chili powder, and salt and pepper and cook for 5 minutes.

Add the mashed beans and cook 10 minutes more over low heat. Remove from the heat and set aside.

Preheat the oven to 350 degrees.

Combine the cornmeal, flour, baking powder, and water in a large saucepan and cook over medium heat until the mixture thickens, stirring constantly with a wire whisk to keep the cornmeal from lumping. Spread half the cornmeal mixture over the bottom of a nonstick baking dish. Spread the bean mixture over the cornmeal mixture, and then add the remaining cornmeal mixture on top, spreading to cover the beans. Bake for 45 minutes or until the cornbread is golden.

Serves 8   PREPARATION TIME: 45 minutes
                              BAKING TIME: 45 minutes

EUROPEAN CUISINE

BROCCOLI VEGETABLE QUICHE

Here is a colorful vegetable pie "real" men, women, and children alike will love.

½ **recipe Sister's Pie Crust (p. 188)**
1 **tablespoon olive oil**
1 **medium onion, diced**
1 **green bell pepper, chopped**
1 **cup chopped broccoli**
1 **cup sliced fresh mushrooms**
1 **pound firm tofu, patted dry with a paper towel**
Pinch of grated nutmeg
½ **teaspoon turmeric**
½ **bunch fresh basil, chopped, or 1 tablespoon dried**
½ **teaspoon salt**

Pepper to taste
½ cup soy milk

Preheat the oven to 425 degrees.
Line a 9-inch quiche pan with the dough and bake for 12 minutes.
Heat the olive oil in a medium saucepan over medium heat, and sauté the onion, green pepper, broccoli, and mushrooms until cooked, about 8 to 10 minutes.
In a blender or food processor, blend the tofu, nutmeg, turmeric, basil, salt, and soy milk until smooth. Stir the vegetables and the tofu mixture together and add pepper to taste.
Pour the batter into the pie crust. Bake for 30 minutes, or until a knife inserted just off-center into the quiche comes out clean.

Serves 4 to 6   PREPARATION TIME: 35 minutes
                                   BAKING TIME: 45 minutes

MUSHROOM-NUT TART

Surprise and impress your friends with this delectable pie. With a moist, nutty crust, it's sure to please even the most discriminating palate!

⅔   **cup slivered almonds**
1   **cup bread crumbs**
½   **cup ground pecans**
1   **small onion, minced**
1   **clove garlic, crushed**
7   **tablespoons margarine, softened**
Salt and pepper to taste
2   **cups sliced fresh mushrooms**
1¼ **cups Tofu Sour Cream (p. 84)**
Grated nutmeg
Paprika

Preheat the oven to 350 degrees.

Reserve a tablespoon of the slivered almonds for garnishing. Mix the bread crumbs, pecans and remaining almonds, onion, garlic, 6 tablespoons of margarine, and salt and pepper. It should hold together like a graham cracker crust.

Press the crust mixture into a 9-inch tart or pie pan and bake until it turns a golden-brown color, about 20 minutes.

Heat the remaining margarine in a large frying pan over medium heat. Sauté the mushrooms for 15 to 20 minutes, or until the liquid has evaporated. Add some salt and pepper to taste. Spoon the mushrooms on top of the semi-baked crust.

With a fork, stir the Tofu Sour Cream, salt, pepper, and nutmeg in a bowl and pour half of this mixture onto the mushrooms, making sure some of the mushrooms show through the cream. Sprinkle paprika over the tart and bake for 10 to 15 minutes.

Garnish the tart with the remaining almonds and serve the remaining sour cream mixture on the side.

Serves 4 to 6   PREPARATION TIME: 40 minutes
                                   BAKING TIME: 30–35 minutes

SAUTÉED TEMPEH WITH LEMON-MUSTARD SAUCE

Luma Restaurant, located near Manhattan's Greenwich Village, prepares this wonderful dish for their patrons. Now it's yours for your special occasions or intimate evenings.

1 **clove garlic**
1 **carrot**
1 **onion**
4 **stalks celery**
2 **tablespoons fresh Italian parsley**
1 **pinch fresh rosemary**

1 **pinch fresh sage**
6 **cups water**
¼ **cup tamari or soy sauce**
4 **ounces tempeh**
¼ **cup unbleached all-purpose flour**
2 **tablespoons vegetable oil**
2 **tablespoons olive oil**
¼ **pound oyster mushrooms**
1 **teaspoon lemon juice**
½ **teaspoon whole grain mustard**
½ **teaspoon Dijon mustard**
1 **tablespoon chives, chopped**

Place the first eight ingredients in a large stock pot. Bring to a boil then lower the heat and simmer for two hours. Strain the stock and discard the waste.

Combine 3½ cups of the stock with the tamari or soy sauce. Bring the stock to a simmer and steam the tempeh in the stock for 20 minutes. Remove the tempeh and allow to cool.

Slice the tempeh into thin long strips and dust it in the flour.

Heat the oil in a medium frying pan over medium heat. Add the mushrooms and tempeh and sauté until tempeh is golden and the mushrooms are well cooked, about 10 to 15 minutes. Remove from the pan.

Keep the pan hot and add ½ cup of vegetable stock and the lemon juice, then add the mustard and chives. Simmer, uncovered, for one minute.

Put the tempeh and mushrooms in a serving dish and cover with the lemon-mustard sauce. Serve immediately.

Serves 2 to 4   PREPARATION TIME: 1 hour
                                   COOKING TIME: 2 hours

RATATOUILLE

Even if you can't live in Paris, at least you can make the world's best ratatouille. Don't forget the French bread and wine.

1   tablespoon olive oil
1   large onion, diced
1   bay leaf
4   tablespoons dry red wine
½   cup tomato juice
4–5 cloves garlic, crushed
1   tablespoon dried basil
½   tablespoon dried marjoram
½   tablespoon dried oregano
Dash of ground rosemary
½   teaspoon salt
½   teaspoon black pepper
1   medium zucchini, sliced
1   green bell pepper, chopped
1   red bell pepper, chopped
1   small eggplant, cut into small cubes
2   large tomatoes, cut into medium wedges
5   tablespoons tomato paste

Heat the olive oil and a little water in a large saucepan over medium heat. Sauté the onion until translucent, about 5 to 7 minutes.

Add the bay leaf, wine, and tomato juice and stir well. Then add the garlic, herbs, salt, and pepper, and mix until well blended. Cover the saucepan and simmer for 10 minutes over low heat.

Add the zucchini and peppers, stir well, cover, and simmer for another 5 minutes. Add the eggplant, tomatoes, and tomato paste and stir again. Cover and continue to simmer until the vegetables are tender, about 8 minutes more.

Serve over rice or with some French bread.

Serves 4 to 5   PREPARATION TIME: 40 minutes

PASTA WITH CHUNKY TOMATO SAUCE

One of the best parts about making this sauce is filling the house with its wonderful aroma.

1½ cups diced onions
¼   cup water or olive oil
¾   cup chopped celery
½   cup chopped green bell pepper
2   cups sliced fresh mushrooms
2   cloves garlic, minced
4   cups chopped fresh tomatoes
3   cups tomato sauce
2   cups tomato puree
1   teaspoon dried oregano
1½ teaspoons dried basil
1   bay leaf
Salt and pepper to taste
1   pound spaghetti or other pasta

Heat the water or olive oil in a large saucepan over medium heat. Cook the onions for 5 to 6 minutes, then add the celery, green pepper, mushrooms, and garlic and cook for an additional 5 minutes.

Add the tomatoes, tomato sauce, and tomato purée and stir until the sauce is well blended. Add the herbs, salt, and pepper and simmer, uncovered, for 30 minutes.

Cook the pasta according to package directions.

Remove the bay leaf from sauce and serve with pasta.

Serves 6   PREPARATION TIME: 1 hour

PASTA WITH OLD WORLD SPAGHETTI SAUCE

This traditional tomato sauce creates pasta perfection!

¼   cup olive oil
1   medium onion, chopped
½   green bell pepper, chopped
8–10 cloves garlic, minced
½   pound sliced fresh mushrooms
2   28-ounce cans crushed plum tomatoes
2   6-ounce cans tomato paste
½   cup dry red or white wine
1   tablespoon minced fresh basil
1   tablespoon minced fresh parsley
1   tablespoon minced fresh oregano
1   teaspoon dried thyme
1   teaspoon crumbled sage
1   teaspoon dried rosemary
2   tablespoons sugar
3   bay leaves
1   teaspoon salt
½   teaspoon pepper
1   pound spaghetti or other pasta

Heat the olive oil in a large saucepan or Dutch oven over medium heat. Add the onion, green pepper, garlic, and mushrooms, and sauté for 2 minutes or until tender.

Add the remaining ingredients, bring the sauce to a boil, then reduce the heat to simmer and cook, covered, for at least 4 hours.

Cook pasta according to package directions. Remove the bay leaves from sauce and serve on hot pasta.

Serves 6   PREPARATION TIME: 20 minutes
                                     COOKING TIME: about 4 hours

TOFU CACCIATORE

This cacciatore is a hearty, spicy dish perfect for a cozy, cold winter night. And since tofu has none of the cholesterol or toxins of chicken, guests needn't worry about having second helpings.

1   pound firm tofu
1   teaspoon olive oil
1   large onion, diced
3   cloves garlic, minced
3   tablespoons tomato paste
¾   cup Vegetable Broth (p. 52)
1   cup canned tomatoes, chopped; or 2 fresh tomatoes, chopped
½   cup sliced fresh mushrooms
½   cup dry white wine
1   teaspoon dried parsley
1   bay leaf
½   teaspoon salt
½   teaspoon ground allspice
¼   teaspoon dried rosemary
¼   teaspoon dried basil
¼   teaspoon black pepper

Drain the tofu and pat dry with a towel. Cut the tofu into ½-inch squares.

Heat the oil in a large skillet over medium heat. Sauté the onion and garlic for 2 minutes. Add the tomato paste, broth, tomatoes, mushrooms, wine, herbs, salt, and spices and stir until thoroughly blended. Bring the sauce to a boil, reduce the heat, and simmer, covered, for 20 minutes, stirring often.

Add the tofu squares and continue to simmer until the tofu is heated through.

Serve the cacciatore with pasta.

Serves 4   PREPARATION TIME: 30 minutes

POTATO GNOCCHI

Once you try these dumplings, you'll never go back to meatballs!

4   **cups cooked potatoes (peeled or unpeeled)**
2   **cups unbleached all-purpose flour**
½   **teaspoon salt**
2   **tablespoons olive oil**

Bring a large pot of water to a boil.

Mash the potatoes dry—that is, do not add any liquid. Stir in the flour, salt and olive oil. Turn the mixture onto a floured bread board or countertop and knead with your hands until you have formed a smooth dough. Add more flour if the dough is sticky.

Divide the dough into 4 pieces and roll each into a long cylinder about 1 inch thick. Cut each cylinder into 1-inch pieces and press your finger into the center of each piece to make an indentation.

Drop a handful of dumplings into the boiling water. They will sink at first, then rise to the surface as they cook. Let boil for another 2 minutes after they have risen to the top, then remove with a slotted spoon. Repeat with remaining dumplings.

Serve hot with Pesto Sauce (p. 157) or Chunky Tomato Sauce (p. 145).

Serves 6 to 8   PREPARATION TIME: 30 minutes

LUSCIOUS LASAGNA

The eggplant and spinach really add substance and flavor to this delightfully unusual lasagna. Whether served as a romantic dinner for two or a large group potluck, it's sure to make the cook look good!

1 tablespoon olive oil
1 clove garlic, minced
1 medium eggplant, diced
2 10-ounce packages frozen chopped spinach, defrosted
8 cups homemade tomato sauce or 1 64-ounce jar commercial
     tomato sauce
1 pound lasagna noodles

Preheat the oven to 375 degrees.

Heat the olive oil in a medium frying pan over medium heat. Sauté the garlic for 2 minutes, then add the eggplant and stir. Cover the frying pan and cook until the eggplant is just tender, about 5 to 7 minutes. Cover the bottom of a 9 × 12-inch baking pan with 2 cups of the tomato sauce, then cover the tomato sauce with 4 or 5 uncooked noodles. Cover this with a thin layer of sauce, then add the cooked eggplant and another thin layer of sauce. Add another layer of noodles followed by a thin layer of sauce, then the spinach and another thin layer of sauce. Add the remaining noodles and sauce. Cover tightly with foil and bake for 45 to 50 minutes. Noodles are cooked when they can be pierced with a fork.

Serves 6 to 8   PREPARATION TIME: 30 minutes
                                   BAKING TIME: 45–50 minutes

TOFU-SPINACH LASAGNA

Lasagna is an ideal choice when you're preparing an intimate dinner for friends. Layered with tofu and spinach, no one will miss the cheese.

½ **pound lasagna noodles**
2 **10-ounce packages frozen chopped spinach, thawed**
1 **pound soft tofu**
1 **pound firm tofu**
1 **tablespoon sugar**
¼ **cup soy milk**
½ **teaspoon garlic powder**
2 **tablespoons lemon juice**
3 **teaspoons minced fresh basil**
2 **teaspoons salt**
4 **cups homemade tomato sauce or 1 32-ounce jar commercial sauce**

Prepare the lasagna noodles according to package directions. Drain carefully and set aside on a towel.

Preheat the oven to 350 degrees.

Squeeze the spinach as dry as possible and set aside.

Place the tofu, sugar, soy milk, garlic powder, lemon juice, basil, and salt in a food processor or blender and blend until smooth.

Cover the bottom of a 9 × 13-inch baking pan with a thin layer of tomato sauce, then a layer of noodles. Follow that with a layer of half the tofu filling and half spinach. Continue in the same order, using half the remaining tomato sauce and noodles and the rest of the tofu mixture and spinach. End with the remaining noodles covered by the remaining tomato sauce. Bake for 25 to 30 minutes, or until tomato sauce bubbles.

Serves 6 to 8   PREPARATION TIME: 30 minutes
                          BAKING TIME: 25–30 minutes

TOFU MANICOTTI

Guests will be surprised to learn that your mouth-watering manicotti is stuffed with tofu—they'll think it's ricotta.

1   **pound manicotti**
2   **pounds firm or soft tofu, patted dry and mashed**
2   **cloves garlic, minced**
½   **cup soy milk**
2   **tablespoons olive oil**
2   **tablespoons lemon juice**
1   **tablespoon sugar**
Salt and pepper to taste
2   **tablespoons minced fresh parsley**
1   **cup chopped fresh spinach (optional)**
4   **cups homemade or commercial spaghetti sauce**

Prepare the manicotti according to package directions. Gently drain and rinse the noodles.

Preheat the oven to 350 degrees.

In a large mixing bowl, stir together the mashed tofu, garlic, soy milk, olive oil, lemon juice, sugar, salt, pepper, parsley, and spinach, if using.

Line a 9 × 13-inch baking pan with 2 cups of the spaghetti sauce. Gently spoon the tofu mixture into each manicotti until they are all full. Place the filled manicotti noodles in one layer on top of the spaghetti sauce. Pour the remaining sauce over the stuffed noodles. Cover the pan tightly with aluminum foil and bake for 30 minutes, or until the sauce bubbles.

Serves 4   PREPARATION TIME: 30 minutes
                                    BAKING TIME: 30 minutes

PASTA E FAGIOLI

You can't go wrong serving this wonderful Italian dish that everyone loves. Make a big batch early for a party and forget worrying about last-minute cooking. A tossed salad and bread are ideal complements.

1   **pound dried great northern beans**
1   **tablespoon salt**
1½ **cups small pasta (ditalini, small shells, broken linguine)**
5   **cups water**
3   **tablespoons olive oil**
1   **large or 2 medium onions, chopped**
3   **cloves garlic, minced**
2   **teaspoons minced fresh basil**
1   **teaspoon dried oregano**
1   **teaspoon salt**
½   **teaspoon pepper**
1½ **tablespoons paprika**
2   **cups tomato sauce (optional)**

In a large pot, soak the beans in water to cover for 8 hours or overnight. Drain and cover the beans with fresh water. Bring the beans to a boil, then simmer, covered, until beans are soft, about 1 to 2 hours.

Add the salt, pasta, and water. Bring to a boil, then simmer until the pasta is cooked.

Meanwhile, heat the olive oil in a medium frying pan over medium heat. Add the onions, garlic, basil, oregano, salt, and pepper and cook until the onion is transparent, about 5 to 7 minutes.

Add this onion mixture to the bean and pasta mixture along with paprika and tomato sauce, if desired. Stir until it is well blended and serve hot.

Serves 8 to 10   PREPARATION TIME: 30 minutes
                                 COOKING TIME: 1½–2½ hours
                                 SOAKING TIME: 8 hours

THREE BEAN PASTA WITH CREAMY SPINACH SAUCE

A delicious satisfying meal.

1 tablespoon olive oil or water
1 large onion, sliced
2 cloves garlic, crushed
1 red bell pepper, chopped
1 teaspoon dried oregano
1 15-ounce can chopped tomatoes, or 2 cups chopped
   fresh tomatoes
½ cup cooked red kidney beans
½ cup cooked navy beans
½ cup cooked chickpeas
Salt and pepper to taste
1 cup small pasta tubes

Sauce

2 tablespoons (¼ stick) margarine
4 tablespoons unbleached all-purpose flour
2 cups soy milk
Salt and pepper to taste
½ teaspoon grated nutmeg
1½ cups finely chopped raw spinach

Heat the olive oil or water in a large saucepan over medium heat. Lightly cook the onion, garlic, and pepper until the vegetables are soft, about 8 minutes. Add the oregano, tomatoes, beans, and chickpeas. Season to taste with the salt and pepper. Cover the saucepan and simmer for 20 minutes.

Prepare the pasta according to package directions. Drain and add to the cooked bean mixture and place this mixture in a shallow serving dish.

To make the sauce, heat the margarine in a medium saucepan over medium heat. Stir in the flour and gradually add the soy milk. Bring to a simmer, stirring constantly, and cook for 2 to 3 minutes, then season with the nutmeg and salt and pepper.

Steam the spinach in 2 tablespoons water for 5 minutes. Drain thoroughly and add to the sauce. Stir until well blended.

Pour sauce over the bean mixture and serve immediately.

Serves 4   PREPARATION TIME: 1 hour

ANGEL HAIR PASTA PRIMAVERA

If you've been living on spaghetti and tomato sauce, this creamy vegetable sauce will add color to your table and reawaken your taste buds.

3   tablespoons olive oil or water
1   medium onion, diced
3   cloves garlic, minced
1   tablespoon dried basil
6   tablespoons unbleached all-purpose flour
3   cups soy milk
¼   cup nutritional yeast
1   small head broccoli, cut into florets and steamed
1   medium carrot, sliced and steamed
½   pound sliced fresh mushrooms
1   cup frozen peas
Salt and pepper to taste
1   pound angel hair pasta

Heat the olive oil or water in a large saucepan over medium heat. Cook the onion, garlic, and basil until the onion becomes translucent, about 5 to 7 minutes. Stir in the flour to make a paste. Slowly add the soy milk, stirring constantly. Stir in the nutritional yeast, then cook over low heat until the mixture thickens.

Steam the broccoli and carrot, and add to the sauce along with the mushrooms and peas. Add salt and pepper to taste, then cook until heated through.

Cook the pasta according to package directions, then serve sauce over pasta.

Serves 6   PREPARATION TIME: 20 minutes

LINGUINE WITH WALNUT SAUCE

Surprise company with this out-of-the-ordinary, out-of-this-world pasta dish. The delicate walnut flavor will warm your palate and wow your friends.

1 cup finely chopped walnuts
3 cups soy milk
2 bay leaves
2 cloves garlic, crushed
2 tablespoons (¼ stick) margarine
3 tablespoons unbleached all-purpose flour
1 teaspoon sugar
Salt and pepper to taste
Fresh parsley
1 pound linguine

Place the walnuts, soy milk, bay leaves, and garlic in a medium saucepan over medium heat and cook, stirring constantly. Just before the mixture boils, remove it from the heat.

Melt the margarine in a large saucepan over medium heat. Gradually add the flour and sugar, stirring until well blended. Cook over low heat for 3 to 4 minutes.

Remove the bay leaves from the sauce, then pour the liquid into the flour mixture and stir well. Simmer for 25 minutes, until thickened. Flavor with salt and pepper.

Cook the linguine according to package directions. Drain well.

Pour the sauce over the linguine, garnish with some fresh parsley, and serve immediately.

Serves 6   PREPARATION TIME: 40 minutes

GARLIC PASTA

Lots of onions and garlic add zest to your pasta.

½–1 pound spaghetti noodles
½ cup virgin olive oil
2 cloves garlic, finely minced
¼ cup finely chopped onion
1 teaspoon salt
Pepper to taste
½ cup toasted bread crumbs

Prepare the pasta according to the package directions.

Heat the oil in a large frying pan over medium heat. Add the garlic and onion and sauté until soft, about 5 minutes. Season with the salt and pepper.

Drain the pasta, reserving ⅓ cup of the cooking water. Pour the cooking water into the oil and garlic mixture and cook over low heat for 1 minute.

In a large mixing bowl, combine the pasta and garlic sauce. Toss, then sprinkle on bread crumbs and serve.

Serves 4 to 6   PREPARATION TIME: 30 minutes

PASTA WITH PESTO SAUCE

This vegan variation on a classic is so easy and delicious, it's sure to become one of your favorites.

1 pound pasta
2 cloves garlic
2 cups packed fresh basil leaves
½ cup pine nuts
¼ cup olive oil
¼ cup hot water
Salt to taste

Cook the pasta according to package directions.

Combine the garlic, basil leaves, and pine nuts in a blender and process on low speed. With the blender running, add the olive oil slowly, followed by the hot water. Add salt to taste and continue processing until the pesto is smooth and creamy.

Drain the pasta and toss in the pesto sauce.

Serves 4 to 6   PREPARATION TIME: 30 minutes

HUNGARIAN STEW

You'll want to keep this recipe handy, to warm up gray winter days.

1 **tablespoon vegetable oil**
1 **medium onion, chopped**
1 **clove garlic, minced**
2 **pounds potatoes (peeled or unpeeled), cut into bite-size chunks**
1 **tablespoon paprika**
1 **tablespoons unbleached all-purpose flour**
4 **cups Vegetable Broth (p. 52) or water**
2 **pounds fresh mushrooms, quartered**
Salt and pepper to taste
½ **cup Tofu Sour Cream (p. 84)**

Heat the oil in a large saucepan over medium heat. Sauté the onion for about 5 minutes, then add the garlic, potatoes, and paprika. Continue cooking and stirring until potatoes are well coated with paprika.

Add the flour to the potatoes and cook for another minute or two.

Add the broth or water and cook over high heat until the mixture boils. Lower the heat, cover the saucepan, and cook for about 20 minutes, or until the potatoes are tender.

Add the mushrooms, salt, and pepper and cook for another 3 to 4 minutes.

Add the Tofu Sour Cream immediately before serving. Ladle into small bowls and serve with a hearty dark bread.

Serves 6   PREPARATION TIME: 40 minutes

STROGANOFF

Pour this versatile sauce over whatever looks good for dinner tonight, and your family will think you labored for hours.

½ cup dry white wine
1 medium onion, chopped
1 clove garlic, minced
1 pound sliced fresh mushrooms
1 tablespoon paprika
2 tablespoons soy sauce or tamari
2 tablespoons Dijon mustard
3 tablespoons unbleached all-purpose flour
2 cups soy milk
1 cup Tofu Sour Cream (p. 84)
Salt and pepper to taste

Heat the wine, onion, and garlic in a saucepan over medium heat until the onion begins to soften, about 5 minutes. Add the mushrooms and continue to cook for 2 minutes.

Add the paprika, soy sauce, and mustard and stir well. Slowly add the flour, stirring constantly, until you have a smooth paste. Add the soy milk, bring to a boil, then turn heat to low and simmer until the mixture begins to thicken, about 5 minutes. Add the Tofu Sour Cream, salt, and pepper and heat thoroughly.

Serve over eggless fettucini, linguini, rice, or baked potatoes.

Serves 4   PREPARATION TIME: 30 minutes

LENTIL SHEPHERD'S PIE

A spicy, hearty blend of potatoes and lentils baked into a savory casserole that's sure to satisfy.

½   **pound lentils, cooked and drained**
1   **small onion, diced**
½   **teaspoon crumbled sage**
½   **teaspoon minced garlic**
Pinch of dried oregano
1   **teaspoon salt, plus more to taste**
Dash of cayenne pepper
3   **large potatoes, cooked and unpeeled**
½–1 cup hot soy milk
Margarine to taste

Preheat the oven to 400 degrees.

In a large mixing bowl, mash the cooked lentils thoroughly and add the onion and seasonings. Put the lentil mixture in a lightly oiled 2-quart casserole dish.

In a separate bowl, mash the potatoes and add the hot soy milk, margarine, and salt. Beat by hand or with an electric mixer, until fluffy.

Spread the mashed potatoes on top of the mashed lentils and bake for 20 minutes, or until potatoes are dry on top. Place the pie under the broiler to brown the top. Serve warm.

Serves 4

PREPARATION TIME: 20 minutes
BAKING TIME: 25–30 minutes

BRAZIL AND CASHEW NUT ROAST WITH CHESTNUT STUFFING

A delightful blend of exotic nuts and spices, this savory loaf is splendid on your holiday buffet table.

2   tablespoons (¼ stick) margarine or water
1   medium onion, finely chopped
1   clove garlic, crushed
5   stalks celery, finely chopped
¾   cup cashews, finely ground
¾   cup Brazil nuts, finely ground
¼   cup flaked millet (see Glossary of Ingredients)
¼   cup bread crumbs
½   cup mashed potatoes
2   teaspoons minced fresh parsley
1   teaspoon dried sage
½   teaspoon dried oregano
¼   teaspoon ground ginger
¼   teaspoon cayenne pepper
¼   teaspoon curry powder
Juice of ½ lemon and rind, grated
Dry wine, vegetable broth, or water
Salt and pepper to taste
1   cup chestnut puree

Preheat the oven to 375 degrees.

Heat the margarine or water in a medium frying pan over medium heat and cook the onion until transparent, about 5 to 7 minutes. Add the garlic and celery and cook 1 minute longer.

Put the mixture in a large bowl with the cashews and Brazil nuts, millet, bread crumbs, potatoes, herbs and spices, lemon juice, and grated rind. Add enough wine, stock, or water to moisten the mixture so it holds together. Season lightly with salt and pepper and mix well.

Put half the mixture in a 8½ × 4½-inch loaf pan. Cover with the chestnut puree, then add the remaining loaf mixture. Bake for 45 minutes.

If desired, serve with Brown Gravy (p. 108) or Chickenless Gravy (p. 111).

Serves 8   PREPARATION TIME: 25 minutes
                                      BAKING TIME: 45 minutes

CASHEW AND CHESTNUT ROAST

Another savory loaf to round out a festive table.

2   tablespoons olive oil or water
2   medium onions, finely chopped
4   cloves garlic, crushed
1   teaspoon dried rosemary
1   teaspoon dried thyme
1¼   cups cashews, ground
5   medium carrots, cooked and mashed
¾   cup whole wheat bread crumbs
1   vegetable bouillon cube dissolved in ¾ cup hot water
3   heaping tablespoons whole wheat flour
3–4 tablespoons water
1   cup chestnut puree
½   teaspoon salt

Heat the oil or water in a medium frying pan over medium heat, and cook the onions, garlic, and herbs until the onions are soft, about 5 minutes. Transfer to a large mixing bowl and add the cashews, mashed carrots, bread crumbs, and bouillon.

In a small mixing bowl, whisk the flour and water together to make a smooth paste, using more or less water as needed. Add to the cashew mixture.

Preheat the oven to 350 degrees. Grease a 8½ × 4½-inch loaf pan or mold.

Place the chestnut puree and salt in a food processor or blender and blend until well mixed.

Spoon half the cashew mixture into the bottom of the loaf pan. Spread the chestnut mixture on top of the cashew mixture, making sure the chestnut mixture stays clear of the sides. Then add the rest of the cashew mixture and press down. Bake for 45 minutes, or until crisp on the outside.

Allow the roast to cool in the pan for 15 minutes, then serve with Brown Gravy (p. 108) or Chickenless Gravy (p. 111).

Serves 8   PREPARATION TIME: 25 minutes
                              BAKING TIME: 45 minutes

10 SIDE DISHES

"People want to help the environment now and going veggie is a constructive way of doing so...."

—PAUL AND LINDA McCARTNEY

Sometimes it's easy to come up with an entree, but you're left wondering what to serve on the side. This chapter is chock full of enticing side dishes like Sautéed Green Beans with Bread Crumbs and Walnuts, Glazed Carrots with a Difference, and Harvest Stuffing to round out meals and give them flair.

Just because we call them side dishes does not mean you have to eat them on the side. Some of these delectable dishes can be a meal in themselves, like our Potato Goulash, Arroz Guisado, and Confetti Quinoa.

BAKED BEANS

Baked beans are picnic-perfect right beside Vegetable Hot Dogs in Blankets (p. 30).

Reprinted with permission from The Peaceful Palate: Fine Vegetarian Cuisine *by Jennifer Raymond.*

1   **pound dried navy beans**
1   **medium red onion, chopped**
1   **15-ounce can tomato sauce**
½   **cup molasses**
2   **teaspoons prepared mustard**
2   **tablespoons distilled white vinegar**
½   **teaspoon garlic powder**
1–2 **teaspoons salt**

Wash the beans, then soak overnight. Discard the soaking water. Place the beans in a kettle and cover with water to 1 inch above the beans. Bring to a boil, then turn the heat to low and simmer, covered, until tender, about 2 to 3 hours.

Preheat the oven to 350 degrees.

When the beans are tender, add the remaining ingredients. Transfer the mixture to an ovenproof 2-quart casserole dish and bake for 2 hours.

Crockpot method: After soaking the beans, place in a crockpot with water to 1 inch above the beans. Cook on high until tender. Add the remaining ingredients and continue to cook on high for 2 hours.

Serves 6 to 8

PREPARATION TIME: ½ hour
COOKING TIME: 2–3 hours
BAKING TIME: 2 hours
SOAKING TIME: 8 hours

BEET CASSEROLE

This casserole "beets" many others hands down for distinctiveness and flavor.

4   **cups peeled and sliced fresh beets**
1   **tablespoon sugar**
¾   **teaspoon salt**
¼   **teaspoon paprika**
1   **tablespoon margarine**
1   **tablespoon lemon juice**
Sliver of fresh ginger
⅓   **cup water**
1   **tablespoon grated onion**

Preheat the oven to 400 degrees.

Layer the sliced beets in a lightly oiled 7-inch baking dish and sprinkle with the sugar, salt, and paprika. Dot the beets with the margarine, then add the lemon juice, ginger, water, and onion. Cover and bake for 30 minutes or until tender. Remove from the oven once during baking and stir well.

Serves 6 to 8   PREPARATION TIME: 10 minutes
                                         BAKING TIME: 30 minutes

ITALIAN-STYLE BROCCOLI

Try this tempting, refreshing broccoli dish.

1 tablespoon olive oil
1 head broccoli, cut into florets
1 clove garlic, minced
2 tablespoons sunflower seeds
3 tablespoons water
Salt and pepper to taste
1 teaspoon fresh lemon juice

Heat the olive oil in a medium frying pan over medium heat, then sauté the broccoli in the oil for 2 minutes. Add the garlic, sunflower seeds, water, and salt and pepper. Cover the pan and cook over low heat until the liquid has evaporated, about 3 to 5 minutes.

Remove pan from the heat and stir in the lemon juice. Serve immediately.

Serves 2 to 4   PREPARATION TIME: 15 minutes

GINGER BROCCOLI

Prevent cancer like a gourmet with this savory broccoli dish.

Reprinted with permission from the Physicians Committee for Responsible Medicine.

1½ pounds broccoli, florets and stems sliced into diagonal pieces
2   teaspoons roasted sesame oil
3   tablespoons tamari

2   teaspoons ground ginger
2   teaspoons brown sugar
4   tablespoons water

In a medium frying pan over medium heat, sauté the broccoli in the sesame oil for about 8 minutes. Combine the tamari, ginger, and sugar, and add to the broccoli. Add water, cover, and simmer for 2 minutes.

Serves 4   PREPARATION TIME: 15 minutes

CABBAGE MEDLEY

Here's a great way to get your servings of vegetables and grains all in one dish and still have room for dessert!

1   tablespoon vegetable oil
1   medium onion, sliced
½   head green cabbage, grated
½   cup water
3½   cups cooked noodles
1   teaspoon salt
½ teaspoon pepper

In a large frying pan, heat the oil over medium heat. Sauté the onion in the oil for a few minutes, then add the cabbage and the water.
    Steam the cabbage mixture, covered, until soft, about 15 minutes. Add the noodles, salt, and pepper. Cook over low heat until the noodles are hot, about 5 minutes more.
    Serve immediately.

Serves 4   PREPARATION TIME: 30 minutes

AUTUMN VEGETABLE PUREE

*Be it a family Thanksgiving or a kick-up-your-heels Halloween mon-
ster bash, this casserole will be the hit of the party.*

2   **medium carrots, peeled and diced**
1   **medium sweet potato, peeled and diced**
1   **turnip, diced**
½   **cup soy milk**
¼   **cup chopped fresh dill**
1   **tablespoon margarine**
Salt and pepper to taste
Grated nutmeg

Preheat the oven to 350 degrees.

Boil the carrots, sweet potato, and turnip in a large saucepan until
very tender, about 20 minutes. Drain the vegetables and transfer to a
food processor or blender and puree.

Stir in the soy milk, dill, and margarine, and season with salt and
pepper to taste. Put in an ovenproof casserole dish and sprinkle
nutmeg over top. Bake, uncovered, for 15 minutes, or until thoroughly
heated.

Serves 4   PREPARATION TIME: 35 minutes

CARROTS WITH A ZING

You'll have 20/20 vision after eating this yummy side dish!

6   **medium carrots, cut into thin strips**
2   **tablespoons grated onion**
2   **tablespoons prepared horseradish**

½ cup Eggless Mayonnaise (p. 85)
1 teaspoon salt
¼ teaspoon pepper
¼ cup water
¼ cup bread crumbs

Preheat the oven to 375 degrees.

Steam the carrots in a small amount of water until tender, about 8 minutes. Drain thoroughly and place in a 6 × 10-inch baking dish.

In a small bowl, mix the onion, horseradish, mayonnaise, salt, pepper, and water. Stir into the carrots and sprinkle with the bread crumbs.

Bake, uncovered, until well heated, about 15 minutes.

Serves 4 to 6   PREPARATION TIME: 20 minutes

GLAZED CARROTS WITH A DIFFERENCE

Vive la différence—*onions! This will look great on your holiday table.*

2 cups peeled and sliced carrots
1 medium onion, diced
¼ cup packed light brown sugar
2 tablespoons (¼ stick) margarine, melted
¼ teaspoon ground cinnamon

Steam the carrots in a small amount of water until tender, about 8 minutes. Drain thoroughly.

In a medium saucepan, combine the carrots, onion, brown sugar, margarine, and cinnamon. Simmer, stirring occasionally, for 15 minutes or until tender.

Serves 4   PREPARATION TIME: 40 minutes

CAULIFLOWER HASH

A twist on cauliflower that makes an excellent side dish.

1 large cauliflower, cut into small pieces
1 tablespoon vegetable oil
1 green bell pepper, chopped
1 small onion, chopped
Salt and pepper to taste
1 tablespoon water

Steam the cauliflower in a small amount of water for only a few minutes (it must be very crisp; just lightly cooked).

In a large skillet, heat the oil on high. Once the oil is hot, add the onion and green pepper and cook until the onion is translucent, about 5 minutes. Turn the heat to medium and cook for another minute, then add the cauliflower. Stir well. Add the salt and pepper and stir well. Add the water and cook a minute longer. Do not overcook; the cauliflower should remain firm.

Serves 8 to 10   PREPARATION TIME: 30 minutes

CREAMED CELERY

Scrumptious topped with crunchy pecans.

4   cups chopped celery
2   tablespoons (¼ stick) margarine
2   cups soy milk
2   tablespoons unbleached all-purpose flour
1   teaspoon salt

¾ **cup pecan halves**
½ **cup bread crumbs**

Preheat the oven to 400 degrees. Lightly oil a 1½-quart casserole.
Boil the celery until tender, about 10 minutes, then drain.

In a medium saucepan over medium heat, melt the margarine and stir in the soy milk and flour. Stir constantly until the mixture thickens and becomes creamy. Add the salt and celery. Pour the mixture into the casserole, top with pecans, and cover with bread crumbs.

Bake for 15 minutes, or until sauce bubbles.

Serves 8   PREPARATION TIME: 20 minutes
                     BAKING TIME: 15 minutes

ORIENTAL GREEN BEANS

Jazz up a meal with these spicy green beans. They'll disappear lickety-split!

1   **pound green beans, trimmed**
1½   **cups water**
1   **tablespoon vegetable oil**
¼   **cup Vegetable broth (p. 52) or water**
2   **tablespoons soy sauce or tamari**
1–2   **teaspoons rice wine or dry sherry**
1   **tablespoon sugar**
3   **cloves garlic, minced**

Heat the water in a wok or large saucepan. Carefully add the beans and steam until tender but crisp, about 8 minutes. Drain and set aside.

In a small bowl, combine the broth or water, soy sauce or tamari, rice wine or sherry, and the sugar, stirring to dissolve the sugar.

Wipe the excess water from the wok or saucepan, add the oil and heat over medium-high heat. Add the garlic and stir-fry for 1 minute. Add the beans and sauce, and cook for 2 minutes, stirring often.

Serve immediately.

Serves 4 to 6   PREPARATION TIME: 20 minutes

SAUTÉED GREEN BEANS WITH BREAD CRUMBS AND WALNUTS

Make a side dish an event. With just a little extra preparation, you can turn green beans into a culinary delight!

2   **tablespoons water**
1   **pound fresh green beans, trimmed**
1   **tablespoon margarine**
1   **tablespoon minced garlic**
½   **cup fresh bread crumbs**
¼   **cup coarsely chopped walnuts**
Salt and pepper to taste

Heat the water in a medium saucepan over medium heat, then cook the beans, stirring constantly, until they are tender but crisp, about 8 minutes.

Turn the heat down to low and stir in the margarine, coating the beans well. Add the garlic and stir a few more minutes. Add the bread crumbs, walnuts, and salt and pepper and serve while still warm.

Serves 4   PREPARATION TIME: 20 minutes

SCALLOPED POTATOES

Cook up a pan of these spuds for your buds, and watch 'em disappear!
(The spuds, that is!)

¼ **cup (½ stick) margarine, melted**
1 **teaspoon salt**
1 **teaspoon pepper**
6 **tablespoons unbleached all-purpose flour**
6 **medium white potatoes, thinly sliced**
1 **medium onion, finely chopped**
2 **cups soy milk**
Paprika
Parsley sprigs, for garnish

Preheat the oven to 350 degrees. With a little of the margarine, lightly grease a 9-inch square baking pan.

Stir the salt and pepper into the flour.

Place ⅓ of the sliced potatoes along the bottom of the pan, followed by ⅓ of the onion, ⅓ of the remaining margarine, and half the flour.

Repeat this layer with ⅓ of the potatoes, ⅓ of the onions, ⅓ of the margarine, and the remaining flour. Top this with the rest of the potatoes, onions, and margarine.

Pour the soy milk slowly into the pan until it almost covers the top layer. Sprinkle with paprika.

Bake for 1½ to 2 hours, until the potatoes are soft and the milk is thick.

Garnish with parsley and serve.

Serves 4   PREPARATION TIME: 20 minutes
                              BAKING TIME: 1½–2 hours

SAGE POTATOES

You don't have to be a Ph.D. to enjoy these delicious sage potatoes.

4 medium potatoes
1 tablespoon olive oil
1 tablespoon ground sage
1 teaspoon paprika
Salt and pepper to taste

Bake for 40 to 60 minutes or microwave for 20 to 30 minutes the potatoes until cooked. Cut, with the skin on, into small chunks.

In a large skillet, heat the oil over medium-high heat. Place the potatoes in the pan and sprinkle with the sage, paprika, salt, and pepper. Stir until well blended. Continue frying, turning the potatoes occasionally, until the desired crispness is achieved, about 20 minutes.

Serves 4 to 6   PREPARATION TIME: 45 minutes–1½ hours

POTATO GOULASH

You'll find potato goulash is an inexpensive, tasty way to fill a hungry belly.

1   tablespoon vegetable oil
2   medium onions, diced
1   cup water
3   potatoes, uncooked, cut into small cubes
2   green bell peppers, chopped
¾   teaspoon dried marjoram
1   teaspoon salt

Heat the oil in a large skillet over medium heat. Sauté the onions in the oil for a few minutes, then add the water, potatoes, and peppers and cook, covered, until the potatoes are soft, about 10 to 15 minutes. Add the marjoram and salt, stir, and serve.

Serves 2   PREPARATION TIME: 25 minutes

OVEN-FRIED POTATOES

Spuds and simplicity seem to go hand in hand. With this one there's no way you can go wrong.

3 large potatoes, washed, dried, and cut into slices about ½-inch wide
1 tablespoon vegetable oil
Salt to taste

Preheat the oven to 475 degrees.
   Place each potato slice on an oiled baking sheet. Turn over to ensure that both sides of the potato are oiled.
   Bake for 15 minutes, then turn each potato slice over and bake for another 15 minutes.
   Sprinkle with salt and serve immediately.

Serves 4   PREPARATION TIME: 15 minutes
                              BAKING TIME: 30 minutes

Variation: For potato chips, slice the potatoes *very* thin and follow the same method.

PERSIAN RICE

Sweet enough to pass for a light dessert!

1	tablespoon margarine
1	cup white or brown rice
1	cup orange juice
1½	cups water
½	cup raisins
¼	cup slivered almonds
¼	teaspoon grated orange peel
1	tablespoon chopped fresh parsley

Melt the margarine in a medium skillet over medium heat. Add the rice and sauté until toasty brown, about 5 minutes. Stir in the juice, water, and raisins. Cover and simmer for 15 minutes if using white rice, 40 minutes if using brown, stirring only twice, until the water is absorbed and the rice is cooked.

Add the almonds, orange peel, and parsley, and serve.

Serves 4   PREPARATION TIME: 20–50 minutes

HARVEST STUFFING

No need to wait until November to enjoy this stuffing.

1	cup shredded carrots
1	cup diced celery
½–1	cup diced onion
¼	cup (½ stick) margarine
1	teaspoon poultry seasoning
¼	teaspoon pepper
½–1	teaspoon salt

8   cups dry bread cubes
2   apples, peeled and finely chopped
½   cup chopped walnuts
1½   cups water or Vegetable Broth (p. 52)

Preheat the oven to 375 degrees.

Melt the margarine in a large skillet over medium heat. Cook the carrots, celery, and onion until tender, about 10 minutes. Stir in the poultry seasoning, pepper, and salt.

In a bowl combine the bread cubes, apples, and walnuts, then add the carrot mixture. Add enough water or broth to moisten, tossing lightly.

Transfer to a 2½-quart casserole dish, cover, and bake for 20 to 30 minutes.

Serves 8 to 10   PREPARATION TIME: 30 minutes
                                    BAKING TIME: 20–30 minutes

SIMPLY DELICIOUS VEGETABLE FRIED RICE

Who needs to order carry-out Chinese when you can make this fried rice so easily at home?

¼   cup soy sauce or tamari
3   tablespoons dry white wine or rice wine
2   tablespoons peanut oil
½   pound soft or firm tofu
2   cloves garlic, minced
1   medium carrot, cubed
1   stalk celery, sliced
1   green bell pepper, chopped
½   cup frozen or fresh peas
4   cups cold cooked rice

Blend the soy sauce and wine and set aside. Heat 1 tablespoon of oil in a wok over medium-high heat. Mash the tofu with a fork and stir-fry for a few minutes. Place the cooked tofu on a paper towel to soak up the excess oil and set aside.

Add the remaining oil to the wok and heat it over medium-high heat. When the oil is very hot, add the garlic and stir-fry for a minute, then add the carrot, celery, green pepper, and peas. Stir-fry for 1 to 2 more minutes, then add the rice and tofu and continue to stir-fry.

Pour the soy sauce mixture over the rice and stir-fry until the rice is heated through, about 5 minutes, stirring frequently.

Serve immediately.

Serves 4 to 6   PREPARATION TIME: 30 minutes

CREOLE-STYLE CHUNKY RICE

Bring the zing of New Orleans to your rice.

2   teaspoons vegetable oil
1   cup diced onion
1   cup finely chopped celery
1   cup finely chopped carrots
¾   cup finely chopped red bell pepper
½   cup finely chopped green bell pepper
2   cloves garlic, minced
1⅓   cups brown rice
1½   teaspoons Creole seasoning
2   tablespoons chopped fresh parsley

Heat the oil in a large skilled over medium heat. Add the onion, celery, carrots, peppers, and garlic and sauté until tender, about 6 to 8 minutes. Set aside.

Cook the rice according to package directions, adding the seasoning. When the rice is done, stir in the vegetables and parsley.
Serve immediately.

Serves 4 to 6   PREPARATION TIME: 45 minutes

ARROZ GUISADO

With garlic, onion, cinnamon, and clove, this is a wonderfully aromatic dish.

1	tablespoon vegetable oil
1	cup brown or white rice
2–3	small tomatoes
1	medium onion
3	cloves garlic
Scant ¼	teaspoon ground cloves
½	teaspoon ground cinnamon
1½	cups Vegetable Broth (p. 52)
1	teaspoon salt
½–¾	cup frozen peas
½–¾	cup frozen hash brown potatoes

Heat the oil in a large skillet over medium heat. Add the rice and sauté until it begins to darken in color, about 5 minutes.

Combine the tomatoes, onion, garlic, cloves, and cinnamon in a food processor and puree until smooth. Add the puree to the rice and cook, stirring, for about 3 minutes. Add the broth and salt. Cover and simmer on low heat until most of the liquid is absorbed, about 30 minutes.

Stir in the peas and potatoes. Cover and steam over low heat until the rice is tender, about 30 to 40 minutes for brown rice, 15 to 20 minutes for white rice.

Serves 6   PREPARATION TIME: 1¼ hours for brown rice
                          1 hour for white rice

CONFETTI QUINOA

As colorful as it is delicious, this grain-based dish, served with a rich tomato sauce or a chunky ratatouille, is an easy part of a hearty meal.

2   **cups water**
1   **cup quinoa, rinsed**
¼   **teaspoon salt**
½   **large onion, diced**
½   **green bell pepper, chopped**
½   **red bell pepper, chopped**
1   **teaspoon vegetable oil**
¼   **cup sliced water chestnuts**
¼   **cup corn, cooked**
Fresh coriander (cilantro), optional

Bring water to a boil and add the quinoa and salt. Cover, reduce the heat to low, and simmer for 15 minutes.

Sauté the onion and peppers in the oil until soft, about 6 to 8 minutes. Add them to the quinoa along with the water chestnuts and corn. Stir until well blended.

Serve garnished with coriander.

Serves 4   PREPARATION TIME: 40 minutes

CASHEW FRIED RICE

A savory side dish that's ideal beside the Vegetarian Burger Loaf, (p. 107).

1   **pound soft tofu, patted dry and mashed**
⅛   **teaspoon turmeric**
1   **teaspoon onion powder**
½   **teaspoon salt**
3   **tablespoons vegetable oil**
5   **cups cold cooked rice**
½   **cup chopped cashews**

Sauce

3   **tablespoons soy sauce or tamari**
½   **teaspoon salt**
1   **teaspoon sugar**
6   **green onions or 3 small yellow onions, chopped**

Mix the tofu, turmeric, onion powder, and salt in a bowl and set aside.

In a medium skillet over medium heat, heat 1 tablespoon of the oil. Add the tofu mixture and cook, stirring constantly for 10 minutes. Remove the tofu from the heat and set aside.

Combine the ingredients for the sauce in a small bowl. Stir to dissolve the sugar and set aside.

Place a dry wok over medium-high heat. When the wok begins to smoke, add the remaining oil, then the onions and rice. Stir-fry for 3 minutes. Pour in the sauce and stir-fry until the rice is heated through, about 5 minutes. Stir in the cashews and the scrambled tofu, and serve hot.

Serves 4 to 6   PREPARATION TIME: 30–40 minutes

BROWN RICE SPLIT PEA-LAF

Cheap eats at their finest. A hearty, lip-smacking side dish that's perfect on cold, winter days.

1   **tablespoon vegetable oil**
1   **medium onion, chopped fine**
2   **cloves garlic, minced**
2   **cups brown rice, rinsed**
3   **cups Vegetable Broth (p. 52)**
3   **tablespoons lemon juice**
½   **cup green split peas**
1   **teaspoon ground cinnamon**
1   **teaspoon ground cumin**
Salt and pepper to taste

In a medium saucepan over medium heat, heat the oil and sauté the onion until golden, about 5 minutes. Add the garlic and rice and stir until coated with the oil. Stir in the broth, lemon juice, split peas, cinnamon, cumin, and salt and pepper to taste.

Bring to a boil, then turn the heat down to simmer. Cover and cook for 45 to 50 minutes, or until all the liquid is absorbed and the rice and peas are tender.

Let stand, covered, 10 minutes, then serve hot.

Serves 6   PREPARATION TIME: 10 minutes

                               COOKING TIME: 1 hour

SPANISH RICE

Spicy Spanish rice coupled with Bean Burritos (p. 132) makes your meal a fiesta!

2   tablespoons vegetable oil
1   cup white or brown rice
1¼   cups crushed tomatoes or tomato sauce
2   cloves garlic, minced
1   small onion, chopped
2⅓   cups Vegetable Broth (p. 52)
¼   cup chopped green bell pepper
¼   cup chopped red bell pepper
1   4-ounce can green chilies

Heat the oil in a large saucepan over medium heat. Add the rice and stir until coated with the oil.

In a food processor or blender, blend the tomatoes or tomato sauce, garlic, onion, and one-third cup of broth until smooth.

Stir the tomato mixture into the rice. Add the remaining broth, cover, and cook over low heat until the liquid has been absorbed and the rice is tender, about 25 minutes for white rice, 45 minutes for brown rice. Stir in the peppers and green chilies. Heat through. Serve immediately.

Serves 8 to 10   PREPARATION TIME: 30–50 minutes

GRAND FINALES

"Nothing will benefit human health and increase the chances for survival of life on Earth as much as the evolution to a vegetarian diet."
—**ALBERT EINSTEIN**

Voilà! On the following pages, you will find the perfect finishing touches for meals—elegant or simple—including creamy-tasting puddings and English trifle, a variety of fillings to fit your homemade or ready-made pastry shells, and homemade cakes. Since they're all minus the heavy cream, fat-laden butter, and cholesterol-packed eggs, there's no need to desert dessert.

For a lunchbox surprise or simply to satisfy a sweet tooth, you'll find plenty of goodies that are sure to leave your taste buds tingling. You can have your cake—and cookies, fudge, and toffee—and eat 'em too, without harming a fellow creature.

PIES AND CRUSTS

SISTER'S PIE CRUST

This simple recipe delivers a light, flaky crust that's perfect for fruit and vegetable pies.

2   cups unbleached all-purpose flour
1   teaspoon salt
¼   cup cold water
⅔   cup solid vegetable shortening

Stir the flour and salt together in a bowl. Take out ⅓ cup of the flour mixture and mix with the cold water to make a paste. Set this aside. With a pastry cutter or fork, cut the vegetable shortening into the remaining flour mixture until the texture becomes "pebbly." Add the paste to the flour-shortening mixture and mix until it can be shaped into a ball. Divide into 2 parts.

Lightly flour your rolling surface (a clean countertop or large wooden board) and your rolling pin. Roll one portion of the pie dough at a time. Roll from the center out, lifting the roller at the end of the dough (rather than rolling back and forth). Roll to a ⅛-inch thickness.

Have an 8- or 9-inch pie pan ready. The rolled dough circle should be at least 2 inches larger than your pie pan. Loosen the pastry from the rolling surface, fold it in half, lift it and lay it in the center of the pie pan. Unfold the pastry, gently work it into the pie pan, and press lightly. Trim off the excess dough with a knife. You can make a design around the edge of the pan using your fingers or a fork.

To pre-bake a pie shell, preheat the oven to 450 degrees. Prick the dough along the edges and on the bottom with a fork. Line with a sheet of foil and weight the dough down with dried beans, half-filling the shell. Bake for 7 minutes. Remove the foil and dried beans, and continue baking for another 3 to 5 minutes. You may freeze the remaining dough.

Makes 2 crusts   PREPARATION TIME: 25 minutes
                                    BAKING TIME: 10–12 minutes

TOFU SWEET POTATO PIE

This sweet potato pie couldn't be easier to make—or better to eat. Just make sure to get yourself a slice before it's all gone.

½ **pound soft tofu**
½ **pound firm tofu**
1 **24-ounce can sweet potatoes, packed in syrup**
2 **teaspoons ground cinnamon**
1 **teaspoon ground ginger**
½ **teaspoon grated nutmeg**
1 **teaspoon salt**
2 **teaspoons vanilla extract**
½ **cup sugar**
1 **9-inch unbaked pie shell (Sister's Pie Crust, p. 188)**

Preheat the oven to 350 degrees.
   Blend the ingredients for the filling in a blender or food processor until free of lumps. Pour into the pie shell and bake for 1½ hours, or until a knife inserted in the center comes out clean.

Serves 6 to 8   PREPARATION TIME: 15 minutes
                                    BAKING TIME: 1½ hours

PUMPKIN PIE

A holiday classic that's enticing anytime.

1¼ **pounds soft tofu**
1   **16-ounce can pumpkin puree**
¾   **cup maple syrup**
¾   **cup sugar**
⅓   **cup unbleached all-purpose flour**
1   **tablespoon ground cinnamon**
1   **teaspoon ground ginger**
1   **teaspoon ground nutmeg**
1   **9-inch unbaked pie shell (Sister's Pie Crust, p. 188)**

Preheat the oven to 400 degrees.

Blend all the ingredients for the filling in a blender or food processor until smooth. Pour the mixture into the unbaked pie shell. Bake for 30 minutes, then turn oven to 350 degrees and bake for another 30 to 45 minutes, or until the filling is set.

Serve warm or cold. For a special treat, garnish with Tofu Whipped Cream (p. 222).

Serves 6 to 8   PREPARATION TIME: 15 minutes
                                        BAKING TIME: 1¼ hours

CHOCOLATE COOKIE CRUST

For those who hate the thought of rolling out a round of flour and shortening, hoping it doesn't break apart in the transfer to the pie plate, this sweet alternative couldn't be easier to make. Use this crust for your favorite unbaked pie filling.

25 vegan chocolate sandwich cookies
⅓ cup margarine, melted

Break up the cookies by hand, then in a blender or food processor, grind the cookies into crumbs. Pour into a mixing bowl, add the melted margarine, and stir. Press the mixture into a 9-inch pie plate. Refrigerate for 30 minutes before filling.

Makes 1 pie crust   PREPARATION TIME: 20 minutes
                                           CHILLING TIME: 30 minutes

GRAHAM CRACKER CRUST

This crust is perfect for many pies, and just right for tofu cheesecake.

8–10 graham crackers (4 sections per cracker)
¼   cup sugar
⅓   cup margarine, melted

Place the graham crackers in a plastic bag and use a rolling pin to make crumbs. (There should be about 1⅔ cups of crumbs.) Pour the crumbs into a bowl, add the sugar and melted margarine to the crumbs, and stir well with a fork.

Pour the pastry mix into a 9-inch pie plate and, using the back of a large spoon, press the mixture into the bottom and sides of the pie plate.

To pre-bake the pie crust, preheat the oven to 375 degrees. Bake the pie crust for 8 minutes, then allow the crust to cool before filling it.

If using an unbaked pie shell, refrigerate the crust for 30 minutes before filling it.

Makes 1 crust　　　　PREPARATION TIME: 15 minutes
　　　　　　　　　　　　BAKING TIME: 8 minutes or chill for 30 minutes

KARIN'S INCREDIBLE CHOCOLATE PIE

Too easy to be true—and a great way to convert tofu-haters.

1¼　pounds soft tofu
¾　　cup semisweet chocolate chips, melted
Sliced kiwi, strawberries, or raspberries
1　　9-inch unbaked Graham Cracker Crust (p. 191) or Chocolate
　　　Cookie Crust (p. 191), chilled

In a blender, puree the tofu to a smooth paste. Add the melted chocolate and blend thoroughly. Pour into the pie crust and chill for at least 2 hours. Garnish with the sliced fruit before serving.

Serves 6 to 8　　　　PREPARATION TIME: 10 minutes
　　　　　　　　　　　　CHILLING TIME: 2 hours

MOM'S VEGAN APPLE PIE

Top off any meal with this updated version of an old-fashioned favorite. Who can resist?

4–5 Granny Smith apples, cored and thinly sliced
⅓ cup margarine, softened
⅓ cup packed dark brown sugar
1 tablespoon ground cinnamon
1 teaspoon grated nutmeg
1 pre-baked 9-inch Graham Cracker Crust (p. 191)

Preheat the oven to 350 degrees.

Place the apples in the crust. Dot with half the margarine. Stir the rest of the margarine into the brown sugar and spices and crumble this mixture on top of the apples.

Bake for 45 to 50 minutes, or until apples are very soft when pierced with a knife.

Serves 6 to 8   PREPARATION TIME: 15 minutes
                         BAKING TIME: 45–50 minutes

SUMMER FRUIT PIE

With four different kinds of fruit, this pie will be the dessert hit of the season!

1½ tablespoons cornstarch
1   20-ounce can juice-packed crushed pineapple
3   fresh peaches, sliced; or 1 20-ounce can sliced peaches, drained
½   cup fresh blueberries
1   pint fresh strawberries, sliced
1   pre-baked 9-inch Graham Cracker Crust (p. 191), cooled
Tofu Whipped Cream (p. 222) (optional)

In a medium saucepan, combine the cornstarch with 3 tablespoons of the pineapple juice. Add the remaining juice and pineapple and cook over medium heat until thickened, about 5 to 7 minutes. Set aside.

Arrange the peaches, blueberries, and strawberries in the crust. Pour the thickened pineapple mixture over the fruit. Refrigerate for 1 hour before serving.

Garnish with Tofu Whipped Cream, if desired.

Serves 6 to 8   PREPARATION TIME: 30 minutes
                                 CHILLING TIME: 1 hour

APPLE COBBLER

One bite of this scrumptious cobbler and your taste buds will be turning cartwheels.

3–4 Granny Smith apples
1   teaspoon ground cinnamon
½   teaspoon ground cloves
½   teaspoon ground allspice

½   teaspoon grated nutmeg
1   cup plus 1 teaspoon sugar
½   cup (1 stick) margarine
1   cup unbleached all-purpose flour

Preheat the oven to 350 degrees.

Grease a 9-inch pie pan. Thinly slice the apples into the pan. Sprinkle the spices and 1 teaspoon of sugar over the apples.

Melt the margarine in a medium saucepan over medium heat. Add the flour and the remaining sugar. Cover the apples with the flour mixture.

Bake the cobbler for 20 to 30 minutes, or until the crust is lightly browned.

Serves 6 to 8   PREPARATION TIME: 15 minutes
                         BAKING TIME: 20–30 minutes

PEANUT BUTTER PIE

A dessert to please all ages, this peanut butter pie will quickly disappear at any gathering!

16 ounces soft tofu
1   cup creamy peanut butter
¾   cup sugar
2   tablespoons soy milk
2   teaspoons vanilla extract
1   unbaked, 9-inch Chocolate Cookie Crust (p. 191), chilled

Combine all the filling ingredients in a food processor or blender and blend until smooth. Spoon into the pie shell. Refrigerate at least 2 hours and serve.

Serves 6 to 8   PREPARATION TIME: 20 minutes
                         CHILLING TIME: 2 hours

CAKES AND FROSTINGS

RUE McCLANAHAN'S CREAMY TOFU CHEESELESS CAKE

Say good-bye to guilt! This dairy-free, eggless cheesecake has all the rich flavor and texture of its fat-packed cousin.

1¼ **pounds soft tofu, patted dry**
1   **pound firm tofu, patted dry**
¾   **cup sugar**
¼   **cup lemon juice**
3   **tablespoons soy milk**
1   **tablespoon vanilla extract**
1   **recipe Graham Cracker Crust (p. 191) pressed into a 9-inch springform pan, baked and cooled**

Preheat the oven to 350 degrees.

Purée the tofu, sugar, lemon juice, soy milk, and vanilla in a food processor or blender until smooth. Pour the mixture into the crust and bake for 50 minutes, or until a knife inserted into the center comes out clean.

Let the cheesecake cool completely before removing the springform and serving.

Serves 6 to 8

PREPARATION TIME: 15 minutes
BAKING TIME: 50 minutes

CHOCOLATE CHEESECAKE

A sweet treat that will cure anyone with tofu anxiety.

1½ pounds firm tofu
1   pound soft tofu
2½ cups sugar
1   cup semisweet chocolate chips
2   teaspoons vanilla extract
1   teaspoon almond extract
1   recipe Graham Cracker Crust (p. 191), pressed into a 9-inch
     springform pan, baked and cooled

Preheat the oven to 325 degrees.

Blend the tofu and sugar in a food processor until smooth. Melt the chocolate chips in the top of a double boiler or in the microwave, then add them to the blended tofu and sugar. Add the vanilla and almond extracts and stir well.

Pour the batter into the baked crust. Bake for 40 to 50 minutes, or until the cheesecake has risen slightly on the sides and the top looks dry.

Cool before cutting. The cheesecake is best if refrigerated for 2 hours before serving, but be sure to let it cool before refrigerating. Remove the springform from the cake before serving.

Serves 6 to 8   PREPARATION TIME: 20 minutes
                              BAKING TIME: 40–50 minutes
                              CHILLING TIME: 2 hours (optional)

APPLESAUCE CAKE

Who says it has to be full of eggs and butter to be moist and delicious? Let them eat cake!

½ **cup (1 stick) margarine**
2 **cups unsweetened applesauce**
2 **cups unbleached all-purpose flour**
1 **cup sugar**
1 **teaspoon baking soda**
1 **teaspoon ground cinnamon**
½ **teaspoon grated nutmeg**
¼ **teaspoon ground cloves**
1 **cup raisins**
1 **cup chopped walnuts**

Preheat the oven to 350 degrees. Grease the *bottom only* of a 9-inch square baking pan.

Melt the margarine in a large saucepan. Remove from the heat and stir in the applesauce, flour, sugar, baking soda, and spices. Add the raisins and nuts.

Pour the batter into the pan and bake for 30 minutes, or until risen and a knife inserted in the center comes out clean.

Serves 9 to 12   PREPARATION TIME: 15 minutes
                                    BAKING TIME: 30 minutes

CHOCOLATE APPLESAUCE CAKE

As easy as pie, and deceptively rich.

3 **ounces unsweetened chocolate, melted**
2 **cups sweetened applesauce, warmed to room temperature**
1 **cup sugar**
2 **cups unbleached all-purpose flour**
1 **teaspoon baking soda**

Preheat the oven to 350 degrees. Grease a 7 × 12-inch baking pan.

Combine the ingredients in the order that they appear and stir well. Spread the batter in the pan.

Bake for 25 minutes, or until the top springs back in the center when lightly pressed.

Serves 9 to 12   PREPARATION TIME: 20 minutes

BAKING TIME: 25 minutes

JOAN'S GRANDMOTHER'S CAKE

This is the luscious cake that has drawn raves from coast to coast at PETA's Animal Rights 101 seminar luncheons. Plenty of chocolate flavor, but no cholesterol.

1½ cups unbleached all-purpose flour
1   cup sugar
3   tablespoons cocoa powder
1   teaspoon baking soda
1   teaspoon vanilla extract
1   tablespoon distilled white vinegar
5   tablespoons oil or melted margarine
1   cup cold water
½   cup (3 ounces) semisweet chocolate chips (optional)

Preheat the oven to 350 degrees.

Using a fork, combine the flour, sugar, cocoa, and baking soda in a 9-inch square baking pan. Stir in the vanilla, vinegar, and oil or margarine.

Pour the water over the mixture and stir well. If you are using the chocolate chips, sprinkle them over the top of the batter, then bake for 30 to 35 minutes or until a knife inserted in the center of the cake comes out clean.

Serves 8   PREPARATION TIME: 15 minutes

BAKING TIME: 30–35 minutes

CHOCOLATE SPICE CAKE

An unusual addition—red wine—adds zing to this chocoholic's dream.

Egg replacer equivalent of 6 eggs
¾ cup sugar
1 cup margarine
1 teaspoon vanilla extract
2 cups unbleached all-purpose flour
1 cup grated bittersweet chocolate
1 tablespoon baking powder
1 teaspoon cocoa powder
1 teaspoon ground cinnamon
¼ cup red wine

Preheat the oven to 350 degrees.

Cream the egg replacer, sugar, margarine, and vanilla, then add the remaining ingredients. Pour the batter into a 9-inch springform pan and bake 40 to 45 minutes, or until a knife inserted in the center comes out clean.

Let the cake cool completely, remove the springform, and serve.

Serves 6 to 8   PREPARATION TIME: 10 minutes
                                  BAKING TIME: 40–45 minutes

CHOCOLATY PUDDING CAKE

Who could turn down chocolaty pudding cake, especially this cholesterol-free wonder? For a special holiday or birthday treat, this cake is delectably unbeatable!

1   cup unbleached all-purpose flour
1   cup sugar
½   cup cocoa powder
2   teaspoons baking powder
½   cup soy milk
2   tablespoons vegetable oil
½   cup chopped walnuts
1¼   cups hot water

Preheat the oven to 350 degrees. Lightly oil a 9-inch square baking pan.

In a large bowl, mix the flour, ½ cup of the sugar, ¼ cup of the cocoa, and the baking powder. Stir in the soy milk and oil, then add the walnuts.

Spread the cake mixture in the baking pan and sprinkle with the remaining ½ cup of sugar and ¼ cup of cocoa. Pour the hot water over the entire cake batter.

Bake for 35 to 40 minutes, or until the cake is set and the chocolate sauce is bubbly.

Serves 6   PREPARATION TIME: 15 minutes
                                    BAKING TIME: 35–40 minutes

LEMON POPPY-SEED CAKE

This is a perfect summertime cake—a light treat without the frosting, a party dish with it.

2–4 lemons
1¼ cups nondairy creamer
2⅔ cups unbleached all-purpose flour
2   tablespoons poppy seeds
3   teaspoons baking soda
¾   teaspoon salt
¾   cup margarine, softened to room temperature
2   cups sugar
Egg replacer equivalent of 3 eggs
½   teaspoon vanilla extract

Preheat the oven to 350 degrees. Lightly oil, then flour two 9-inch square or round cake pans.

Grate 4 teaspoons of lemon rind and squeeze ¼ cup fresh lemon juice. Combine the lemon juice with the nondairy creamer and set aside.

Combine the flour, poppy seeds, baking soda, and salt and set this aside.

With an electric mixer set at medium speed, beat the margarine with the sugar and grated lemon rind for 5 minutes. Beat in the egg replacer and the vanilla. Reduce the speed of the electric mixer to low and beat in the flour mixture one-third at a time, alternating with one-third of the creamed mixture at a time. Beat until smooth.

Pour the batter into the prepared cake pans. Bake for 30 minutes, or until a toothpick stuck in the center comes out clean. Cool on a rack for 10 minutes.

Remove the cakes from the pans and let cool completely. Leave unfrosted or frost with one of your favorite vegan frostings.

Serves 12   PREPARATION TIME: 30 minutes
                                BAKING TIME: 30 minutes

CARROT CAKE

Carrot cake is one of those yummies that are easy to make without all the added eggs and milk. This recipe is one of the PETA staff's all-time favorites.

Reprinted with permission from The Peaceful Palate: Fine Vegetarian Cuisine *by Jennifer Raymond.*

2   **cups grated carrots**
1½   **cups raisins**
2   **cups water**
½   **cup vegetable oil**
1¼   **cups maple syrup**
1½   **teaspoons ground cinnamon**
1½   **teaspoons ground allspice**
½   **teaspoon ground cloves**
1½   **teaspoons salt**
3   **cups unbleached all-purpose or whole wheat pastry flour**
1½   **teaspoons baking soda**
¾   **cup chopped walnuts**

Preheat the oven to 350 degrees. Grease a 9-inch square baking pan.

In a large saucepan over medium-low heat, simmer the carrots and raisins in the water until the raisins are soft, about 7 to 10 minutes. Remove from the heat and add the oil, maple syrup, cinnamon, allspice, cloves, and salt. Stir and let cool.

In a large mixing bowl, combine the flour, baking soda, and walnuts. Add the carrot mixture and mix until well blended.

Pour batter into baking pan and bake for 45 minutes to 1 hour, or until inserted knife comes out clean.

Serves 9 to 12   PREPARATION TIME: 20 minutes
                                        BAKING TIME: 45 minutes–1 hour

NUT TORTE

Any dinner guests claiming to be too full for dessert will change their tune when you present this heavenly torte.

¾   **cup margarine**
2¼ **cups sugar**
Egg replacer equivalent of 3 eggs
3   **tablespoons fresh lemon juice**
Pinch of salt
2½ **cups unbleached all-purpose or all-purpose flour**
2½ **teaspoons baking powder**
¾   **cup soy milk, plain or vanilla**
2   **cups chopped walnuts or almonds**
½   **cup vegan marzipan (see Glossary of Ingredients)**

Preheat the oven to 400 degrees.

To prepare the dough, cream the margarine with ¾ cup sugar until fluffy. Add the egg replacer, lemon juice, and salt and mix well. Add the flour and baking powder, and mix until a soft dough is formed.

Place two-thirds of the dough on a sheet of plastic wrap. With a rolling pin, roll the dough into a circle about 11 inches in diameter. Invert the dough into a 9-inch springform pan. Peel the plastic wrap off the dough and press the dough into the bottom and up the sides of the pan. Trim the edges if needed. Roll the remaining dough into a circle about 9 inches in diameter and set aside. This will be used to top the torte.

To prepare the filling, stir 1 cup of sugar in a large heavy saucepan over low heat until the sugar is dissolved. Increase the heat and boil the sugar until it turns a caramel color. Add the soy milk (which will bubble vigorously) along with the nuts and the rest of the sugar. Cook over high heat, stirring constantly, for 5 minutes. Remove from the heat and beat the marzipan into the mixture. When it is well mixed, pour it into the cake pan and put the rolled-out dough on top.

Bake the torte until golden brown, about 35 minutes. Cook completely before removing the springform.

Serves 6 to 8   PREPARATION TIME: 40 minutes
                                  BAKING TIME: 35 minutes

YELLOW CAKE

Baking a cake from scratch is easy with this basic recipe; top with berries or tofu ice cream for a special treat, or decorate with colored icing for Valentine's Day or the Fourth of July!

½   cup (1 stick) soft margarine, softened
1   cup sugar
Egg replacer equivalent of 4 eggs
1⅜ cup sifted unbleached all-purpose flour
½   teaspoon baking powder
Soy milk as needed

Preheat the oven to 325 degrees. Grease the bottom only of a 8-inch square pan.

Cream the margarine with an electric mixer until smooth. Add the sugar gradually. Add the egg replacer and mix well. Add the sifted flour and baking powder and stir. If the mixture is too dry, add a few drops (up to ¼ of a cup) of soy milk.

Spread the mixture in the prepared pan and bake for 30–40 minutes. Allow the cake to cool and frost with your favorite vegan frosting, if desired.

Serves 6 to 8   PREPARATION TIME: 25 minutes
                                   BAKING TIME: 30–40 minutes

APPLE TORTE

You can't go wrong with this torte, and your guests will never guess how easy it is to make.

Batter for Yellow Cake (p. 205)
2   pounds apples, preferably Delicious, peeled, cored, and sliced
½   teaspoon ground cinnamon
2   tablespoons sugar
½   cup slivered almonds, roasted
Confectioners' sugar

Preheat the oven to 400 degrees. Cover the bottom and sides of a 9-inch springform pan with waxed paper.

Mix the cake according to the directions, then spread on the bottom of the pan with a spatula. Arrange the apple slices on the cake mixture, then sprinkle with the cinnamon and sugar.

Bake the cake for about 25 to 30 minutes, or until a knife inserted to the center comes out clean. (To be sure not to burn the cake, check early; it may finish sooner, depending on the thickness of the dough.)

Sprinkle cake with the roasted almonds and a light layer of confectioners' sugar. After the cake is completely cooled, cut into slices.

Serves 6 to 8   PREPARATION TIME: 20 minutes
                                   BAKING TIME: 25–30 minutes

TRIFLE

This dessert is no trifle; it's a chef d'oeuvre that will have your guests oohing and aahing—both before and after they take a bite!

Batter for Yellow Cake (p. 205)
Vanilla Pudding (p. 212)
½ cup cream sherry or your favorite liqueur
¾ cup raspberry jam
1 small can peaches, drained and sliced
2 medium bananas, sliced
Tofu Whipped Cream (p. 222) or commercial nondairy whipped topping
Toasted slivered almonds, for garnish

Preheat the oven to 325 degrees. Grease a 9 × 13-inch cake pan.

Prepare the cake batter according to the recipe, then pour the batter into the prepared pan (the batter should be less than 2 inches high in the cake pan) and bake for 25 to 30 minutes.

Let the vanilla pudding cool (do not refrigerate, however).

When the cake has cooled, cut it into 1 × 3-inch pieces. Line the bottom and sides of a 2½ quart glass serving bowl with the cake pieces. Moisten the cake with the sherry or liqueur and spread the raspberry jam over the cake. Add the sliced peaches and bananas. Pour the pudding over the fruit and chill in the refrigerator.

Before serving, top with the Tofu Whipped Cream or nondairy topping and decorate with toasted almonds.

Serves 8   PREPARATION TIME: 30 minutes
                              BAKING TIME: 25–30 minutes

TIRAMISÙ

Dessert-time decadence guaranteed to wow the uninitiated with the wonders of tofu. It's irresistible!

Batter for Yellow Cake (p. 205)
1 cup espresso or other very strong coffee
Tofu Whipped Cream (p. 222)
1 tablespoon cocoa powder

Preheat the oven to 325 degrees. Grease a 9 × 13-inch baking pan.

Prepare the cake batter according to the recipe, then pour the batter into the prepared pan (the batter should be less than 2 inches high). Bake for 25 to 30 minutes or until a knife inserted in the center comes out clean.

Cool cake on a rack, then cut the cake into thirds and place one slice into a 8½ × 4½-inch loaf pan. Pour one-third of the espresso or coffee over the cake and cover with one-third of the Tofu Whipped Cream. Repeat this process with the remaining cake slices, espresso or coffee, and Tofu Whipped Cream.

Refrigerate for 1 hour before serving. Sprinkle the top with the cocoa powder before serving.

Serves 6   PREPARATION TIME: 1 hour
                              BAKING TIME: 25–30 minutes
                              CHILLING TIME: 1 hour

TOFU FROSTING

An excellent icing for Carrot Cake (p. 203).

½   **pound soft tofu, patted dry**
2   **tablespoons lemon juice**
3–4 **tablespoons confectioners' sugar**
½   **teaspoon vanilla extract**

Place all the ingredients in a blender or food processor and puree until very smooth.

Frosts one 9-inch cake   PREPARATION TIME: 15 minutes

VANILLA FROSTING

You'll be tempted to "taste-test" this frosting so many times you won't have enough left for a cake. But that's okay; it's so quick and easy to prepare you can whip up another bowlful in no time.

¾   **cup confectioners' sugar**
¾   **cup (1½ sticks) margarine**
⅛   **cup vanilla soy milk**

Combine ingredients in a mixing bowl. Using an electric mixer, blend until creamy. The consistency of the frosting may vary. Add more sugar, margarine, or soy milk as needed.

Frosts one 9 × 13-inch cake   PREPARATION TIME: 10 minutes

LEMON FROSTING

This sweet frosting is easy to make and complements Lemon Poppy-Seed Cake (p. 202) particularly well.

2   **cups confectioners' sugar**
¼   **cup (½ stick) margarine, softened**
2   **tablespoons soy milk**
Juice and grated rind of one lemon

With an electric mixer set at low speed, cream the sugar and margarine. Beat in the soy milk and lemon juice. Stir in the lemon rind.

Frosts 1 large cake   PREPARATION TIME: 20 minutes

CHOCOLATE ICING

Chocolate frosting is the perfect topping for Yellow Cake (p. 205); or for a double chocolate sensation, top Joan's Grandmother's Cake (p. 199) with this rich chocolate delight.

3   **ounces unsweetened chocolate**
2   **teaspoons margarine**
¼   **cup hot water**
2   **cups confectioners' sugar**
1   **teaspoon vanilla extract**

Over very low heat, or in a microwave on low power, melt the chocolate and margarine together. Transfer to a mixing bowl and add the hot water. Slowly stir in the sugar until the frosting is creamy (you may not need the entire 2 cups of sugar). Add the vanilla and stir. Allow the frosting to cool.

Frosts 1 large cake   PREPARATION TIME: 20 minutes

Variation: For Mocha Frosting, substitute hot coffee for the hot water.

PUDDINGS AND CUSTARDS

BREAD PUDDING

You don't have to be a character in a Charles Dickens novel to enjoy bread pudding. And all you need to make it is seven ingredients, and a little time.

4   **cups cubed day-old whole wheat or white bread**
3   **cups soy milk**
¾ **cup sugar**
1   **tablespoon vanilla extract**
1   **teaspoon ground cinnamon**
1   **cup raisins**
½ **cup chopped almonds**

Preheat the oven to 350 degrees.

Put the bread into a 9-inch square baking pan or 2½ quart casserole dish. Stir the remaining ingredients together in a separate bowl and pour over the bread. Stir to mix. Bake 30 minutes. Serve warm or cool.

Serves 6   PREPARATION TIME: 15 minutes
          BAKING TIME: 30 minutes

212 PETA AND INGRID NEWKIRK

DARK CHOCOLATE MOUSSE

When you really want to treat yourself, this smooth dessert will help you do it in style!

1   **pound soft tofu**
½   **cup cocoa powder**
¼   **cup carob powder**
6   **tablespoons sugar**
½   **cup soy milk**

Place all the ingredients in a blender or food processor and puree until creamy. Pour the mousse into parfait glasses or individual dessert bowls and chill.

Serves 6   PREPARATION TIME: 10 minutes
                              CHILLING TIME: 1 hour

VANILLA PUDDING

Who would think that five simple ingredients could be combined to make such a smooth, special dessert? The proof is in this low-fat, zero cholesterol pudding!

⅓   **cup sugar**
3   **tablespoons cornstarch**
⅛   **teaspoon salt**
2   **cups soy milk**
1   **teaspoon vanilla extract**

Mix the sugar, cornstarch, and salt in a large saucepan. Gradually blend in the soy milk, stirring constantly to avoid lumps.

Cook the mixture over low heat, stirring constantly until thickened. Cook for an additional 2 to 3 minutes, stirring now and then.

Remove the pudding from the heat and add the vanilla. Let cool for 10 minutes, stirring now and then. Pour the pudding into a large serving dish or individual serving dishes and chill until firm, about 2 to 3 hours.

Makes 4 servings   PREPARATION TIME: 40 minutes
                                   CHILLING TIME: 2–3 hours

COCONUT PUDDING

The tropical taste of coconut makes this dessert extra special. You'll be amazed that a dessert so easy to prepare can taste so heavenly.

1   **pound soft tofu**
½   **cup sugar**
1½   **teaspoons vanilla extract**
½   **cup shredded coconut**

Whip the tofu, sugar, and vanilla extract in a blender or food processor until stiff and creamy. In a bowl, fold the coconut into the tofu mixture.

Pour the pudding into parfait glasses or individual dessert bowls and chill. For an extra treat, serve topped with chocolate sauce.

Serves 4   PREPARATION TIME: 10 minutes
                                   CHILLING TIME: 1 hour

RICE PUDDING

The perfect pudding for a winter night. You won't mind baking it for three hours—your kitchen will smell delightful.

½ **cup white rice**
4 **cups soy milk**
2 **teaspoons vanilla extract**
1 **teaspoon ground cinnamon**
Dash of nutmeg
¼ **cup sugar**
½ **cup raisins**

Preheat the oven to 275 degrees.
   Mix all the ingredients in a bowl and place in a 1½ quart lightly oiled ovenproof dish. Bake, covered, for 3 hours, or until the pudding sets.

Serves 6   PREPARATION TIME: 10 minutes
                              BAKING TIME: 3 hours

TEMBLEQUE (Coconut Milk Custard)

Smooth, sweet, and irresistible.

⅓ **cup cornstarch**
⅓ **cup sugar**
½ **cup soy milk**
2 **cups coconut milk, unsweetened**
Ground cinnamon, for garnish

In a medium saucepan, mix all the ingredients with a wire whisk or electric mixer set at low speed until well blended (make sure there are no lumps).

Bring the mixture to a boil over medium heat, stirring constantly. Turn the heat to low and continue to cook, stirring constantly, until the mixture thickens. Beat with a wire whisk or electric mixer to ensure that it is smooth.

Transfer the custard to a bowl or individual serving dishes and refrigerate until set. Sprinkle with cinnamon before serving.

Serves 4 to 6   PREPARATION TIME: 20 minutes

COOKIES AND SWEETS

SCOTCH SHORTBREAD

Company is coming and the coffee is brewing. Shortbread pieces hit the spot when a sophisticated, mildly sweet treat is in order.

1   **cup (2 sticks) margarine, at room temperature**
½   **cup sugar**
1   **teaspoon imitation butter flavor**
2   **cups unbleached all-purpose flour**

Preheat the oven to 275 degrees.

In a medium mixing bowl, cream the margarine and gradually add the sugar. Stir in the imitation butter flavor. Work in the flour ½ cup at a time. On a floured bread board or countertop, knead the dough for at least 10 minutes, using small amounts of flour to prevent it from sticking.

Pat and roll the dough so it is ½-inch thick. Cut the dough into rectangles or diamonds with a knife, and transfer the pieces to an ungreased cookie sheet, leaving adequate space (about ½ inch) between each cookie. Prick each piece 2 or 3 times with a fork.

Bake for 30 minutes, or until the cookies become slightly golden brown around the edges. Allow to cool before sampling.

Makes 30 to 40 cookies   PREPARATION TIME: 25 minutes
                                  BAKING TIME: 30 minutes

CHOCOLATE-DIPPED CRESCENTS   .

A delectably sweet, nutty treat that's more than just a cookie.

¾   **cup (1½ sticks) plus 1 teaspoon margarine**
½   **cup confectioners' sugar**
1½   **teaspoons vanilla extract**
1¾   **cups unbleached all-purpose flour**
¾   **cup chopped walnuts or pecans**
½   **cup semisweet chocolate chips**

Preheat the oven to 350 degrees.

Mix ¾ cup margarine with next 4 ingredients thoroughly in the order given. Pull off small handfuls of the dough and roll them into ½-inch cylinders about 1-inch long. Shape the cylinders into crescents. Place the cookies on a cookie sheet. Bake for 15 minutes or until lightly browned, then let cool.

While the cookies are cooling, melt the chocolate chips and remaining teaspoon of margarine together in a medium saucepan over very low heat. Remove from the heat.

Once the crescents have completely cooled, dip one end of each crescent cookie into the chocolate mixture and place on a foil-covered cookie sheet. Chill in a refrigerator until chocolate hardens, about 30 minutes.

Makes 36 crescents

PREPARATION TIME: 30 minutes
BAKING TIME: 15 minutes
CHILLING TIME: 30 minutes

CINNAMON RAISIN BARS

These irresistible bar cookies will be a hit at any bake sale, but be sure to make an extra batch for folks at home.

1   **cup confectioners' sugar**
¼   **teaspoon ground cinnamon**
1   **tablespoon soy milk**
¼   **cup granulated sugar**
1   **tablespoon cornstarch**
1   **cup plus 2 tablespoons water**
2   **cups raisins**
½   **cup (1 stick) margarine**
1   **cup packed dark brown sugar**
1¼   **cups unbleached all-purpose flour**
½   **teaspoon baking soda**
1½   **cups rolled oats**

Mix the confectioners' sugar, cinnamon, and soy milk in a large mixing bowl, and set aside.

Combine the granulated sugar and cornstarch in a heavy saucepan. Stir in 1 cup water and the raisins, and cook over medium heat until it becomes thick and bubbly, about 10 minutes. Set aside and let cool.

Preheat the oven to 350 degrees. Grease a 9 × 13-inch baking pan.

Cream the margarine and brown sugar together with an electric mixer. Add the flour and baking soda, and mix well. Stir in the oats and remaining tablespoon of water. Mix until crumbly.

Put half the oat mixture into the pan and spread the raisin filling on top. Sprinkle the rest of the oat mixture on top of the raisin mixture and pat smooth.

Bake for 35 minutes, or until bars set. Let cool, then drizzle with cinnamon icing and cut into bars.

Makes 12 to 16 bars   PREPARATION TIME: 1 hour
                                   BAKING TIME: 35 minutes

TIGER BALLS

Novelist D. H. Lawrence once said, ''A tiger is striped and golden for his own glory.'' These chocolaty peanut butter treats are striped and golden for your taste buds' glory.

2   **cups vegan cookie crumbs or graham cracker crumbs**
½–1   **cup peanut butter (creamy or crunchy)**
3½   **cups confectioners' sugar**
1   **cup (2 sticks) margarine, melted**
1   **cup semisweet chocolate chips**

Line a cookie sheet with aluminum foil.

In a large mixing bowl, combine the crumbs, peanut butter, sugar, and margarine and mix thoroughly with a wooden spoon. Roll this mixture into 1-inch balls, place on the cookie sheet, and chill in the refrigerator.

Meanwhile, place the chocolate chips in a small plastic sandwich bag and melt carefully (do not overheat) in a microwave. (If you prefer, melt the chips in a small bowl over hot water, then pour the melted chocolate into the sandwich bag.)

Snip off a tiny corner (about ¹/₁₆ inch) of the baggie and squeeze chocolate from this corner, drizzling thin "tiger stripes" of chocolate over the chilled cookies.

Return cookies to the refrigerator and chill until the chocolate is firm, about 30 minutes.

Makes 3 to 4 dozen balls   PREPARATION TIME: 20 minutes
                                     CHILLING TIME: 30 minutes

COCONUT ORANGE BALLS

Perfect for parties and picnics, these sweet nuggets are a snap to make. The tropical taste may induce daydreams of a faraway island paradise.

1½ cups vegan cookie crumbs
2   cups confectioners' sugar
½   cup (1 stick) margarine, melted
¾   cup orange juice concentrate, thawed
1   cup chopped nuts (optional)
¾   cup flaked or shredded coconut

In a large mixing bowl, combine the cookie crumbs and the confectioners' sugar. Add the margarine and orange juice. Mix thoroughly and add the nuts, if using.

Shape the mixture into 1-inch balls. Roll in the coconut, place on a cookie sheet, and chill for 1 hour.

Makes 3 to 4 dozen balls   PREPARATION TIME: 20 minutes
                                     CHILLING TIME: 1 hour

PEANUT BUTTER DROPS

A slight variation on an old favorite, these delectable drops are full of oats and peanutty flavor.

½ cup (1 stick) margarine
2 cups sugar
½ cup soy milk
3 cups rolled oats
5 tablespoons peanut butter (creamy or crunchy)
1 teaspoon vanilla extract

Line a cookie sheet with foil or waxed paper.

Melt the margarine in a large saucepan over low heat. Add the sugar and soy milk, and increase the heat to medium. Bring the mixture to a boil for 1 minute. Remove from the heat; add the oats, peanut butter, and vanilla; and mix vigorously.

Drop the mixture by spoonfuls onto the cookie sheet and let stand until firm.

Makes 2 to 3 dozen drops   PREPARATION TIME: 20 minutes

EASY FUDGE

If you thought fudge had to be dairy-rich, think again! There's not a drop of moo-juice (no milk or butter) in this recipe, yet it's surprisingly easy to make, unlike most traditional fudge recipes, which require a candy thermometer and lots of luck. Makes a great, quick gift when someone needs to be cheered up or wants to celebrate.

6   tablespoons (¾ stick) margarine
3½ cups confectioners' sugar

½   cup sifted cocoa powder
1   teaspoon vanilla extract
¼   cup soy milk
1   cup chopped nuts (optional)

Lightly grease a 5 × 9-inch loaf pan using a little of the margarine.

Place the remaining margarine, sugar, cocoa, vanilla, and soy milk in a heatproof mixing bowl or the upper part of a double boiler.

Place the bowl or boiler over simmering water and stir until smooth. Add the nuts if desired.

Pour the mixture quickly into the prepared pan. Chill thoroughly and cut into squares.

Makes 2 to 3 dozen squares   PREPARATION TIME: 15 minutes

                                      CHILLING TIME: 1 hour

CHOCOLATY PEANUT BUTTER KRISPIES

A classic combination—peanut butter and chocolate—in a chewy, crunchy bar. A perfect lunchbox treat!

1 cup sugar
1 cup corn syrup
1 cup peanut butter
6 cups crispy rice cereal
2 cups chocolate chips

Cook the sugar and corn syrup in a medium saucepan over medium heat until bubbly. Remove from the heat and add the peanut butter and cereal and mix well.

Spread the mixture in a 9 × 13-inch pan.

In a double boiler, melt the chocolate chips and pour over the cereal mixture. Chill until firm and cut into squares.

Makes 2 dozen squares   PREPARATION TIME: 15 minutes

CHILLING TIME: 1 hour

DESSERT TOPPINGS AND SUMMER FARE

TOFU WHIPPED CREAM

Research on humans has shown that vanilla is one of several scents that have a relaxing effect on people, so take a good whiff of this yummy whipped cream if you're feeling frazzled!

1   **pound soft tofu**
1   **tablespoon vanilla extract**
¼   **cup sugar**
¼   **cup soy milk**

Combine tofu, vanilla, and sugar in a blender or a food processor and process until smooth. With the machine running, gradually add the soy milk through the feeder cap. Refrigerate until serving time. It will keep for a week, but can also be frozen.

Makes 1⅓ cups   PREPARATION TIME: 15 minutes

ENGLISH BUTTER-FREE TOFFEE TOPPING

This gooey treat is a great topping for your favorite tofu "ice cream."
It's so sinfully delicious you may try to talk yourself out of eating
some, but don't—those extra sit-ups are worth it.

1½ cups (3 sticks) margarine
1⅞ cups sugar
1   cup sliced almonds
1   cup semisweet chocolate chips, melted
½   cup finely chopped almonds or walnuts (optional)

Lightly grease the bottom and sides of a 9 × 13-inch or larger pan or cookie sheet with raised edges.

Melt the margarine in a large heavy saucepan over low heat. Add the sugar and boil, stirring constantly, until the mixture reaches 260 degrees (measured with a candy thermometer). Add the sliced almonds and continue boiling until the mixture reaches 300 degrees.

Pour the hot mixture carefully into the pan. Allow the toffee to cool to lukewarm, then spread with the melted chocolate chips. If desired, chopped almonds or walnuts can be sprinkled on top of the chocolate.

When completely cool, spoon this over your favorite vegan frozen dessert or over bread pudding.

Makes 6 cups   PREPARATION TIME: 30 minutes

AMBROSIA

Delightfully cool and delicious, ambrosia is ideal for the hot and hazy days of summer.

1 cup each of chopped fresh pineapple, apples, and oranges; sliced strawberries; and organic grapes
½ cup shredded coconut
1 tablespoon cornstarch
6 tablespoons lemon juice
3 tablespoons sugar
3 tablespoons orange juice
½ cup soft tofu, pureed
2 teaspoons grated orange rind
1 teaspoon poppy seeds (optional)

In a large bowl, toss the fruit and coconut until well blended. Refrigerate.

Combine the cornstarch with the lemon juice in a medium saucepan and stir until well blended. Place the saucepan over low heat and add the sugar and orange juice. Cook, stirring constantly, until the mixture thickens, about 5 to 10 minutes. Remove the saucepan from the stove and allow to cool thoroughly.

Fold the pureed tofu, orange rind, and poppy seeds into the juice mixture and chill for at least 1 hour.

Immediately before serving, pour the dressing over the fruit and serve.

Serves 6 to 8

PREPARATION TIME: 25 minutes
CHILLING TIME: 1 hour

SUMMER SORBET

This cold, fruity dessert is a heavenly ending to a meal. Try making it with a different fruit each time until you find your favorite versions.

1 cup sugar
1½ teaspoons cornstarch
2 cups water
2 cups pureed fruit (strawberries, blueberries, peaches, raspberries, pineapple, honeydew, watermelon)

Dissolve the sugar and cornstarch in the water in a large saucepan over low heat, then boil until thick, like syrup, about 10 minutes. Remove from the stove and let cool.

When the sugar syrup is completely cooled, add the pureed fruit and mix well. Place the sorbet in a plastic container and freeze uncovered until it is solid, about 8 hours.

Cut the mixture into small chunks, place in a food processor, and whizz for 2 minutes until soft and fluffy. Put the mixture back into the plastic container and refreeze for about 6 hours.

Makes 1½ quarts PREPARATION TIME: 1 hour
FREEZING TIME: 14 hours

GLOSSARY OF INGREDIENTS

Acorn Squash—Winter squash about four to six inches wide, oval to acorn shape with a grooved and ridged surface. Dark green color with variations of orange and yellow. In season, it is available in all produce departments of regular grocery stores.

Almond Extract—An alcohol extract of macerated kernels used for flavoring. Available in regular grocery stores.

Amchur (Amchoor)—A powder made from sour, unripe mangos. It gives food a slight sweet-and-sour flavor. Available in Indian grocery stores.

Asafetida—A brown resin used in small quantities in Indian cooking for its flavor. Available in Indian grocery stores.

Bamboo Shoots—Buds of bamboo harvested as soon as they appear above ground and used as a vegetable, particularly in Chinese cuisine. They are sold canned in the United States. Available in Chinese and most regular grocery stores.

Basmati Rice—A fine-grained, aromatic rice. Available in Indian grocery stores.

Bay Leaf—The dried leaf of a bay laurel tree, used as an herb to flavor food but should not be eaten. Available in regular grocery stores.

Brown Rice—Long-grain or short-grain rice that is unmilled (the hulls are still on). Available in health food and some regular grocery stores.

Bulgur Wheat—Steamed, dried, and cracked whole wheat. It is commonly used in Middle Eastern cuisine. Cracked wheat may be substituted for bulgur, since they both have the same texture and protein quality. Available in health food and some regular grocery stores.

Cannellini—Also called white kidney beans. Large creamy white beans popular in Italian dishes. They are available canned and can be found in international foods sections of regular grocery stores.

Capers—Greenish buds and young berries of the caper plant, which are pickled. Used as a condiment in cooking. Available in the gourmet section of regular grocery stores.

Caraway Seeds—The aromatic pungent-tasting seed of the caraway plant. It is like cumin in appearance and flavor. Available in regular grocery stores.

Cardamom—An aromatic spice, generally sold in the pod but also ground. Available in regular grocery stores.

Carob Powder—A dark powder made from the fruit of the carob tree. It has a flavor similar to chocolate. Available in health food stores.

Cayenne Pepper—A hot red pepper, dried and ground. Available in regular grocery stores.

Chana Masala—A blend of spices (cumin powder, coriander powder, garam masala, and amchur) used in Indian dishes. Available in Indian grocery stores.

Chestnut Puree—Pureed chestnuts and water. Comes in a can and is available in the gourmet section of most regular grocery stores.

Chickpea Flour—Flour made from dried chickpeas. Used in India and the Middle East as a thickener for sauces and in batters. Available in Indian, Middle Eastern, and some health food stores.

Chickpeas (Garbanzo Beans)—A round, beige bean very popular in Middle Eastern and Indian cooking. Available dried or canned, in Middle Eastern, Indian, and regular grocery stores.

Chili Powder—A blend of dried powdered chili pepper, cumin, oregano, and other spices. Mildly hot. Available in regular grocery stores.

Cilantro—Also called Chinese parsley, it is an herb used in many ethnic dishes. It is the parsleylike leaves of fresh coriander. Available in Indian, Chinese, and some regular grocery stores.

Cloves—The dried flower buds of a Southeast Asian evergreen. They are brown in color and have a woodlike texture. Available in regular grocery stores.

Coconut Milk—Not to be confused with the liquid found in the center of the coconut, the milklike liquid that has been strained from grated coconut boiled in water. Available in Asian grocery stores and in the gourmet section of some regular grocery stores.

Coriander, Fresh—See CILANTRO.

Coriander Seeds—Ripened, dried fruit of coriander used for flavoring in many Middle Eastern and Indian dishes. Sold both whole and ground. Available in regular grocery stores.

Cornmeal—Ground corn kernels. The texture of the meal can range from coarse to fine. Available in regular grocery stores.

Cornstarch—A white powder made from corn and used as a thickening agent. Available in the baking section of regular grocery stores.

Creole Seasoning—A blend of salt, pepper, red pepper, garlic, and other seasonings. Available in most grocery stores or in gourmet food stores.

Cumin—Seed of a plant related to the parsley family, with a slightly bitter flavor. It is frequently used in Indian and Middle Eastern curries. Sold whole and ground. Available in regular grocery stores.

Curry Powder—A combination of spices, specifically coriander, turmeric, fenugreek, cumin, and chili. Frequently used in Indian recipes. Available in regular grocery stores.

Dry Onion Soup Mix—Dehydrated onions, cornstarch, salt, sugar, oil, and so on. Most dry onion soup mixes do not have any meat, egg, or dairy products, but make sure you read the label. Available in regular grocery stores.

Egg Replacer—Combination of starches and leavening agents used to replace the binding qualities of eggs in baking. Made primarily from potato starch. Available in health food and some regular grocery stores.

Eggless Mayonnaise—Mayonnaise made out of vegetable oils as opposed to eggs. Available in health food stores but you can also make your own mayonnaise; see recipe on page 85.

Fennel Seeds—The seed of the fennel flower, commonly used as a condiment. They have a flavor similar to anise, but milder. Available in regular grocery stores.

Flaked Millet—Millet that has been flaked; see MILLET. Available in some health food stores.

Garam Masala—A basic, ground curry spice mixture. Available in Indian grocery stores.

Gluten Flour—Extracted from wheat flour, and available as a type of flour, gluten is the high-protein substance that allows dough to hold together. Available in health food stores.

Granny Smith Apples—A green, crisp, and somewhat sour apple. When in season, available in produce departments of all regular grocery stores.

Great Northern Beans—A large version of the navy bean that absorbs flavors well. Available in regular grocery stores.

Green Split Peas—Split, skinned, dried peas that are medium green in color. Available in regular grocery stores.

Horseradish—The grated root of the horseradish plant. It has a hot and spicy radishlike flavor. Available in regular grocery stores.

Hot Chili Oil—Vegetable oil flavored with fresh chili peppers or chili pepper juice. Available in Chinese grocery stores.

Hot Sauce—A liquid mixture of hot red pepper, vinegar, salt, and seasonings. Used in barbecue sauces and chili dishes. Available in regular grocery stores.

Imitation Butter Flavor—Consists of water, flavorings, and color and is completely dairy-free. Available in regular grocery stores.

Imitation Chicken-Flavored Powder—A blend of soy beans, dehydrated vegetables, flour, oil, yeast, and spices. Used to season gravies, stuffings, roasts, and soups. Available in health food stores.

Kidney Beans—A red bean in the shape of a kidney. Available dried or in cans in regular grocery stores.

Kiwi Fruit—A fruit native to Australia and New Zealand. It is light brown on the outside and light green on the inside, with little crunchy, edible black seeds in the center. It is a very juicy, sweet fruit. Available in most regular grocery stores.

Lentils—Tiny, flat, lens-shaped legumes that come in two colors, green and red. They can be cooked like peas or beans. Available in regular grocery stores.

Liquid Smoke—A liquid seasoning made from roasted hickory wood. Gives food a smoky flavor. Available in most regular grocery stores.

Margarine—A vegetable fat usually made from soy beans, corn, and/or other vegetables. Make sure you read the label of commercial margarines because most contain whey. Commercial vegetable oil "spreads" taste like margarine and usually do not contain whey. Available in regular grocery stores.

Marzipan—An almond and sugar paste. Make sure you read the label of commercial marzipan, as it may contain egg whites or dairy products. Available in gourmet and international food stores.

Millet—The grain of a hardy annual grass containing more protein and iron than any other grain. Available in health food stores.

Molasses—A sweetener made from the residue left when cane sugar is refined. It is brown in color, very thick, and rich in minerals. Available in regular grocery stores.

Mung Bean Sprouts—Crunchy, white, sprouted mung beans. Used in Chinese stir-fries and salads. Available in most regular and Chinese grocery stores.

Mung Dahl Beans (split and husked)—The yellow interior of the mung bean. Available in Indian grocery stores.

Navy Beans—Also called white beans or haricot beans. They are a small, white, all-purpose bean that absorb other flavors well. Available in regular grocery stores.

Nori—A green sea vegetable mostly grown in Japan. It is sold in sheets. Available in Japanese, Chinese, and health food grocery stores.

Nutritional Yeast—A food yeast grown in a molasses solution. It comes in yellow flakes or powder. Available in health food stores.

Oregano Seeds—Dried seeds from the oregano plant. Available in Indian grocery stores.

Pinto Beans—Beige beans with maroon spots. They are native to India and are used in many Mexican dishes. Available in regular grocery stores.

Pita Pockets—Middle Eastern flat bread that can be opened into a pocket to be filled with sandwich ingredients. Available in regular grocery stores.

Poppy Seeds—Gray-blue, small, round seeds. They give foods a pleasant, nutty flavor. Available in regular grocery stores.

Poultry Seasoning—A combination of herbs and spices (no "poultry")—specifically, black pepper, salt, coriander, savory, sage, thyme, marjoram, celery salt, and parsley flakes. Available in regular grocery stores.

Puff Pastry Shells—Frozen, ready-made shells available in most regular grocery stores. They usually do not contain eggs or dairy products, but check the label to make sure.

Quinoa—A round, sand-colored, high-protein grain with a mild, nutty taste and a light texture. Available in health food stores.

Rolled Oats—Hulled oats steamed and then flattened by being passed between rollers. Available in regular grocery stores.

Seasoned Salt—A combination of salt, herbs, and spices. Available in regular grocery stores.

Silken Tofu—A high-protein food made from soybean curd. Silken Tofu comes in both a firm and a soft variety. It has a soft, custardlike texture, very smooth when blended, and is a good dairy substitute. Available in some regular grocery, Chinese grocery, and health food stores.

Soy Sauce—The salty, reserved liquid from fermented soy beans, used as a condiment. Available in regular grocery stores.

Soy Milk—A sweet milk made from soy beans that have been ground, soaked, and filtered. Available in health food and some regular grocery stores.

Tahini—A ground sesame seed paste with a slightly bitter and nutty flavor. Available in Middle Eastern grocery stores and in most regular grocery stores.

Tamari—Naturally fermented soy sauce, available in a variety of forms including wheat-free and low-sodium. Available in Chinese and some regular grocery stores.

Tarragon—An herb that has a delicate, lemon-licorice flavor. Available in regular grocery stores.

Tempeh—A chewy, meatlike food made from fermented soybeans. It has a nutty taste and can be used in almost any recipe that calls for meat. Available in health food stores and Chinese grocery stores.

Tofu, Firm, Chinese-style—A very high-protein food made from soybeans. This variety of tofu is the hardest and is a good meat substitute. It looks a little like ricotta cheese. Available in most regular grocery, Chinese grocery, and health food stores.

Tofu, Soft, Chinese-style—A very high-protein food made from soybeans. This variety of tofu is softer in texture, and is a good dairy substitute. It also looks a little like ricotta cheese. Available in most regular grocery, Chinese grocery, and health food stores.

Tofu, Silken, Japanese-style—See SILKEN TOFU.

Tofu Hot Dogs—Hot dog–shaped links made from soybeans and other nonmeat ingredients. The texture and flavor are similar to meat hot dogs. Available in health food stores.

Turmeric—A member of the ginger family. When ground it is bright yellow. It is used to color and flavor Indian curry dishes. Available in regular and Indian grocery stores.

TVP (Texturized Vegetable Protein)—Granules made predominantly from soy beans. Gives a hearty, chewy texture to chili, soup, casseroles, spaghetti sauce. TVP is generally fortified with Vitamin B^{12}. Available in health food stores.

Vanilla Extract—A flavoring extract made by soaking vanilla pods in a mixture of water and grain alcohol. Available in regular grocery stores.

Vegan Chocolate Sandwich Cookies—Chocolate cookies that have no egg, dairy products, honey, or their derivatives in their list of ingredients (e.g., Hydrox chocolate sandwich cookies). Available in some regular grocery stores.

Vegan Cookie Crumbs—Vegan cookies that have been ground or crumbled. Vegan cookies are any cookies that have no egg, dairy products, honey, or their derivatives in their list of ingredients. Available in some regular grocery stores.

Vegan Cornbread Stuffing—Cornbread stuffing mix that has no meat, egg, dairy products, honey, or their derivatives in their list of ingredients. Available in most regular grocery stores.

Vegan Sour Cream—See page 84.

Vegetable Broth—Can be made by dissolving a vegetable bouillon cube in water or using the broth of a clear vegetable soup, like the one on page 52.

Vegetarian Burger—A combination of wheat gluten, food starch, soybean oil, salt, onions. It is a vegetable protein product that comes in a can and is available in some regular grocery stores.

Wasabi—A powder that can be made into a strong, green Japanese horseradish paste. Sold in Japanese and some regular grocery stores.

Water Chestnut—A dark-skinned and chestnut-size tuber that grows in the water. It is used sliced as a vegetable in China. Available fresh in Chinese grocery stores and canned in regular grocery stores.

Watercress—A green, spicy, pungent herb with leaves that taste like pepper. It can be eaten in salads or soups or sautéed as a vegetable. Available in most regular grocery stores.

White Beans—A generic term for all types of white beans, such as cannellini, great northern, and navy beans.

Yeast Extract—An alcohol extract made from yeast, combined with salt, vegetable extract, and spices. Used as a bread or toast spread in England. Available in gourmet and health food stores.

INDEX

> Note: Recipe titles appear in boldface type. For descriptions of ingredients, please refer to the Glossary of Ingredients on pages 227–236.